DECK IDEAS YOU CAN USE

CREATIVE DECK DESIGNS FOR EVERY HOME & YARD CHRIS PETERSON

Creative Publishing international

MINNEAPOLIS, MINNESOTA
www.creativepub.com

Creative Publishing
international

Copyright © 2011
Creative Publishing international, Inc.
400 First Avenue North, Suite 400
Minneapolis, Minnesota 55401
1-800-328-0590
www.creativepub.com
All rights reserved

Printed in China

10 9 8 7

President/CEO: Ken Fund
Group Publisher: Bryan Trandem

Home Improvement Group

Associate Publisher: Mark Johanson
Managing Editor: Tracy Stanley
Creative Director: Michele Lanci-Altomare
Art Direction/Design: Brad Springer, Kim Winscher,
   James Kegley
Production Managers: Laura Hokkanen, Linda Halls

Author: Chris Peterson
Page Layout Artist: Mighty Media
Copy Editor: Ingrid Sundstrom Lundegaard

Contents

Introduction

No deck design is perfect for everyone. Every home, yard, and homeowner is unique. That's why your ideal deck is particular to you. It should accommodate the way you want to use and enjoy your outdoor space, and it should complement both your house and the particular contours of your yard. Design your perfect deck and you improve your home and the way you live.

That deck design begins with function. What do you want to use it for? Are you looking to revel in the liquid luxury of a spa tub, or make your pool more accessible? Do you love to cookout for friends and family? Or are you just hoping to create a platform for stargazing and unwinding after a busy day at the office? No matter what purpose you intend for the structure, that use will radically affect the design you choose.

Of course, decks are highly visible structures, so your deck design needs to also take into account the architecture of your home and the contours of your yard. Any deck should be a handsome addition to a house—or at least blend inoffensively—and should be a natural partner to the terrain of your yard.

Combine your ideal function and form in the deck design, and you'll wind up with your perfect deck. It may be a multilevel structure with comfortable sitting areas and a fire pit for large outdoor parties. Or it might be a single-level surface surrounding your pool, with a small outdoor kitchen off to one side to serve your penchant for cooking out almost every night in good weather. Regardless of what your perfect deck design entails, you'll find all the ideas and inspiration you'll need in the pages that follow.

Choose from among the different decking materials, select a configuration that makes sense for your house, your yard and your budget. Then pick from a bevy of features big and small—from hot tubs to built-in seating and planters—that will make the deck your own. It's true that no single deck design is perfect for everyone, but there is a perfect deck design for you. And it's waiting for you somewhere in this book.

The unmistakable beauty of real redwood provides the perfect backdrop for a luxurious outdoor spa. The large tub has been positioned as the centerpiece of the deck, a place where the homeowners can unwind after a long day, looking out over an expertly landscaped yard. The "clear heart" rated boards used here not only offer an unrivaled appearance relatively free of knots and imperfections, they also resist rot and insects.

Although they require more involved design and construction (and significantly higher cost), multilevel decks are great for serving multiple purposes with one structure. The upper level of this deck has been divided into a dining section and casual seating area defined by built-in planters. The spa tub is more naturally located on the ground level of the deck, where it's weight is more easily supported, and the tub itself is visually linked with the pool.

One of the requirements of a successful deck design is that it merge fluidly with the structure of the house. This modest, ground-level backyard deck tucks in attractively next to a bump-out in the architecture. The white vinyl decking and railing not only provide low-maintenance deck surfaces, they also match the home's siding. Use low-growing foundation plantings, like the plants bordering the perimeter of this deck, to further blend a deck into its surroundings.

You'll rarely go wrong with a deck design that takes its cues from the shape of the house. The semicircular shape of this deck mimics the arcing brick bump-out, creating an inviting semi-circle that opens out into the yard. The deck visually nests into an inside corner, and the color of the composite decking perfectly complements the house siding and trim. An arbor overhead provides dappled shade.

A deck doesn't need to be elevated to be a powerful graphic element. This deck sits at surface level, creating a handsome area right next to a pool. Entirely waterproof, the composite decking is ideal for a site such as this, and the neutral color allows the alluring blue of the pool to dominate the backyard scene. Always have an idea of what you want to showcase—garden features, a pool, a view, or the deck itself—before you settle on a final deck design.

A multilevel deck is a great way to make a severely sloped yard more usable. The design of this deck features dual octagons that create a wealth of seating in a small amount of space. A handsome stairway provides access to the more level portion of the backyard. Notice that the more structurally important handrail on the staircase is supported with iron balusters, while the balusters on the top deck rail are impact-resistant Plexiglas.

Two-tone color schemes can spice up even the simplest of decks. Both colors in this deck—created of composite materials—complement the weathered siding on this coastal home. Rather than using a freestanding pergola, the pergola joists have been attached to the house itself, creating a better visual flow from the main structure out onto the deck.

If you live in the midst of nature, you can go one of two ways with your deck design: blend in or stand out. Here, the homeowner has chosen the former, opting to build a modest lower deck around an existing evergreen, and using synthetic decking the exact color of the home's siding. Sturdy, simple, built-in benches make this the perfect area to sit, reflect, and simply enjoy the forested location.

Use a poolside deck as a fantastic opportunity to go beyond the staid traditional stone patio surface. The deck around this pool spells luxury with a capital L, including two built-in pergolas that define and separate sitting and dining areas. The rest of the deck is left uncovered to allow for unrestricted sunbathing, and to exploit an incredible wooded vista on the other side.

Distinctive architecture calls for a distinctive deck. The signature look of this Tudor-style home would have been poorly served by a traditional front deck; this surprisingly ornate custom redwood deck answers the call perfectly. Curved and detailed balusters, a gabled pergola-style overhang, and lattice skirting all add to a Swiss-village look that enriches the home's exterior appearance. With fast-growing plants trained up the support posts, the newly installed deck fits so well with the house that it looks like part of the original construction.

A deck can easily be the star of the landscape. In this case, however, the stunning, oversized spa tub is the main character. The color of the deck was chosen to blend the space with surrounding rock-strewn jungle landscaping. The directional pattern of the boards was specifically designed to draw the eye toward the spa.

Use a deck to turn a beautiful view into a usable sanctuary. This bilevel lower deck transformed a large, densely forested, hilly backyard into a secluded outdoor hideaway perfect for recharging your batteries and entertaining well away from the pressures of the outside world. Subtle but effective wired-in lighting makes the space enjoyable night or day, and complementary browns in the border boards, level transition and field of the deck provide a measure of visual interest while blending into the surroundings.

You can make even a small deck seem special with the right materials and architectural details. The designer of this deck achieved a stunning look with the grain and color of the ipe hardwood used for the decking. He accented that beauty with finely detailed post molding that replicates the appearance of milled footing.

Curving shapes are eminently pleasing to the eye, and often suit landscaped yards better than a square or rectangle would. creating a pleasing shape, the designer of this deck used white composite legs for the benches, making them stand up visually as The benches also provide an obvious edge border, creating a more defined and formal area between house and lawn.

Designing a deck for your house often means marrying old and new to avoid the deck looking like it was tacked on. This older brick house is perfectly complemented by the new composite deck, which was designed as an extension of the existing porch. A border of lighter colored boards establishes the connection with the porch, and the color of the decking and railings work well with the brick facade.

Contrast can be a powerful tool in designing a deck. It's all about how and where you use contrasting materials and colors. The unique appearance of this redwood decking is set off by sparkling, bright white railings and stair risers. White is a great accent or detail color for most decks, creating a sharp, clean look against most types of decking. White risers are practical as well, providing a visual depth indicator to prevent tripping when the sky is overcast.

Pools and decks are natural combinations, and the deck can often serve as a whole-yard solution. Decking most of the backyard around this pool and spa provides a nice feel underfoot and lets the pool be the center of attention. The composite decking is waterproof, solving the problem of potential rot inherent in such a wet location.

Deck builders make use of modern technology in the form of hidden deck fasteners and low- or no-maintenance synthetic decking. This deck uses both, with curving fascia boards that attractively conceal the structural components of the deck, and a built-in privacy screen around the spa tub that will never need to be painted or refinished. This deck will look just as new years from now, and requires very little maintenance on the part of the homeowner.

Decking Materials

The biggest choice you'll make in designing a deck is the material used to build it. The decking material you pick will affect how easy or hard your deck is to build, how much time you spend maintaining it, how long it lasts, and the final cost. But perhaps more importantly, the substance you choose will—to a large extent—determines the deck's appearance.

You'll select from four basic options: pressure-treated wood; synthetics and composites; softwoods including cedar, redwood, and pine; and exotic hardwoods such as ipé, tigerwood, and cambara (often grouped under the general term "ironwood" for their hardness and durability). Start with the look of different options. You'll be living with the deck for a good long time, and it should ideally complement the colors and textures around your home. Your choice will also be affected by how much maintenance you're willing to do; a composite deck requires little or none, while a cedar or redwood deck may entail yearly staining and sealing to avoid deterioration. Of course expense will be a big part of the decision as well. These materials range wildly in cost. The difference between building a deck of pressure-treated wood (often the least expensive option) and high-end mahogany can be thousands of dollars.

Some choices will naturally pop to the top of list. Where moisture is a constant—such as around a pool, spa, or in a wet part of the country—high-quality composite decking will hold up well without rotting. If your yard is a densely landscaped naturalistic setting, the alluring natural appearance of a hardwood or softwood may make these your preferred materials. Choose the right decking material for your tastes and physical site, and you'll enjoy years of a great-looking outdoor recreation area with a minimum of hassle.

Homeowners choose redwood for its sheer beauty. Given the relatively high price, it's smart to design the deck to show off the wood's loveliness as much as possible. This small backyard deck showcases the material grandly, using it in the lattice skirting, decorative top rails and post caps, and layered fences on the far side. Those details—and the redwood color and grain—create a captivating appearance far out of proportion to the deck's small footprint.

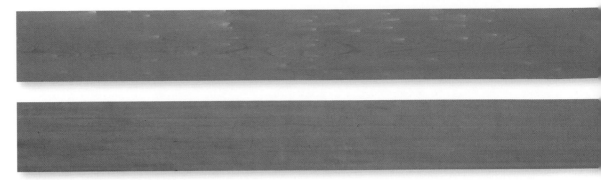

Redwood was the original decking material, chosen for its incredible color and enthralling grain patterns. There are 30 different grades of redwood but only a handful are used for decks. The better the grade, the fewer visible imperfections such as a knots, and the more resistant the wood will be to insects and moisture-related problems. Look for clear all heart (shown above), clear, or clear heart grades, to construct a high-quality, lasting deck.

Redwood is a natural choice for pool decking, because heart grades resist moisture and rot, and any redwood takes stains and finishes as well as, or better than, any other softwood. This elegant deck provides a walkway around a pool, complementing a stone border and adding fascinating detail with grain and deep color that draws the eye.

Redwood

Redwood can be sealed and left its natural red, stained, allowed to weather, or even painted, as it has been here. An oil-based deck paint effectively seals and protects the wood, and in this case, colors the deck a gray that perfectly complements the color of the house's siding. A bright white pergola and railings provide some visual pop, and ensure that the deck doesn't fade into a ho-hum neutral look.

Your decking and built-in deck fixtures do not necessarily need to be the same grade, same material, or finished to match each other. Variation and contrast add visual interest in large decks, and this outdoor space makes good use of that principle. The pergola and built-in planters and seating were all sealed to retain the eye-catching original color of the wood. The decking has been left unfinished, the color fading into gray as the wood ages.

Nowhere is a redwood deck more at home than under a copse of trees on an untamed woodsy hillside. This deck provides wonderful outdoor space on a previously unusable hillside, and seems to meld into the earth tones surrounding it. The redwood is well suited for this application, as one of the strongest softwoods. The underlying support structure was built of less attractive and less expensive pressure treated lumber. Redwood fascia boards and lattice skirting ensure the alluring color and patterns of the redwood dominate.

Cedar

A majestic elevated deck is proof that you don't necessarily need to rely solely on the grain and color of cedar to make a beautiful deck from the wood. Cedar takes both stain and paint well. White-painted fascia and support beam trim pieces look crisp and clean, and perhaps even better than they would left natural. Cladding support beams is one way to turn a functional part of the deck into arresting design element.

Cedar is constantly fascinating underfoot. With surface patterns and a rich tan color unlike any other wood. The designer of this deck added even more visual interest by running the boards of the lower deck on diagonal. Cutting boards for diagonal placement is a way to add flair to the deck. Cedar is so beautiful that builders usually use same wood for the railings as well as the surface.

Lighter and browner than redwood, cedar is, however, similar in that it is naturally rot and insect resistant. It is lightweight and easy to work with, and doesn't check or split. Left natural, as it has been on this deck, it will eventually weather to a gray similar to aging redwood.

One of the advantages of cedar is that it complements many different siding materials and colors. It also blends in well with just about any type of landscaping. The simple linear design for this elevated deck works well with the uncomplicated architecture of the house and the expanse of lawn below. The beautiful cedar grain stands out even in side view.

Pressure-Treated Wood

Pressure-treated pine is ideal for ground-level decks where moisture and insects could be concerns. The wood is also sturdy enough for support structures such as the modest pergola and seating that border this deck. Regardless of the material, though, designing a deck to sit at an angle to the house is a great way to make what might otherwise be a plain surface more visually interesting.

If you're using lower-grade pressure-treated decking, you can improve the appearance by staining or painting, as the homeowner did with this deck. By choosing a shade very similar to the siding, the deck blends seamlessly with the house. A built-in bench adds style, and running boards in the three different directions on the two different levels give the structure a restrained flair.

Pressure-treated pine provides a low-cost and—as shown here—potentially handsome material for complicated deck constructions. The recreational platform in this photo includes built-in seating with a louvered pergola, planter boxes, detailed fencing, and lattice skirting, at a fraction of what hardwood construction would have cost.

A light stain is the ideal finish for pressure-treated southern pine, highlighting the interesting grain pattern. Although railings are often crafted of different wood, or stained in a different shade, the builder of this bilevel deck stained all the wood the same. The effect gives the look continuity, making it easy on the eye.

The elegantly fine-grained cumaru hardwood used in this dining deck is perfectly accented by chic glass railing inserts. Cumaru is not only beautiful, but also dense and strong enough to last several decades. Reputable suppliers sell only cumaru from certified sustainable forests, making this an environmentally responsible choice for the homeowner searching for a gorgeous deck material.

Cumaru is an incredibly hard and strong wood, with a dense structure that resists moisture, insects, rot, and mold. It's an ideal wood for high-traffic stairs like these leading from this main back door to a cumaru deck. The hardwood can be left unfinished, in which case it will age to a lovely gray. Sealed, it will keep the dynamic, deep brown shown here.

Garapa, also known as Brazilian ash, offers the lovely honey color shown here. Clear heart is the most common quality used, ensuring that no knots or imperfections mar the golden yellow surface. This deck has been finished in a clear, penetrating, oil-based sealer that maintains the original color. Notice that the builder used steel post-and-beam supports that are visually unobtrusive and tie the deck and pergola to the modern style of the house.

Sharp, clean white railings and fascia boards create a compelling contrast to the chocolate brown of ipé hardwood decking.
The combination helps show off the fine grain and lush coloration of the hardwood. The railings and fascia boards are made from composite materials; using less expensive materials for details like these goes a long way toward cutting the overall cost of a hardwood deck.

Ipé hardwood combined with a dramatic deck design equals an arresting look that's hard to top. Ipé was used in this deck, including the steep terraces and angled stairs, to contrast the modern architecture's siding. The color of the hardwood complements splashes of brown in the stone used for the patio surface. The shapes of the deck structure interestingly contrast the lower surface.

When you have a stunning hardwood to work with, the deck design itself doesn't necessarily have to be complex. This simple, single-level deck with built-in bench pops out against the green grass because of the captivating tigerwood used to build the deck. The wood's stunning surface and signature dark stripes create amazingly beautiful patterns.

Board direction and the fascinating pattern of tigerwood work together to make this deck's surface an attention grabber. Low-maintenance tigerwood is less expensive than other hardwoods, but features a deep golden or reddish brown base color with dark brown or black striping throughout. This deck makes great use of the wood's patterns with boards running toward a diamond inlay centerpiece. Create this sort of visual interest and you may find guests on the deck spending more time looking down than looking out at the view.

Composites

Composite decking provides a textured, splinter-free surface, making the material ideal for an exposed sun deck such as this. Most composites and PVC decking are prone to some modest fading under direct sun exposure, but manufacturers formulate their colors specifically to allow for some fading without overly obvious change in the color.

Composite decks can be installed with hidden fasteners such as the one shown here. The fasteners allow you to create a clean look on the deck surface, with boards spaced closely together and no visible screw or nail heads showing to mar your deck surface.

High-quality composites come in a range of colors, textures, and grain patterns. Many mimic expensive hardwoods, such as this composite deck, which looks convincingly like a tropical ironwood such as garapa. Even with modest fading, this deck will look like a much more expensive wood structure for decades to come, all with the minimal maintenance of two or three cleanings a year.

Composites

Quality composite decking is resistant to mold, rot, moisture infiltration, and splintering. All of which makes it a great decking choice for a multi-purpose structure such as this backyard retreat, where water will be splashed and bare feet are the order of the day. Most composites are also easy to clean, making any table spills a breeze to deal with. And, as this picture shows, the material is no slouch in the looks department either.

Many composite decks are designed to be monocolor because all the pieces are made of the same material. The look is very clean and creates a unified deck look, to which small accent details—like the post cap lights shown here, which illuminate the spa tub mounted on its own concrete footing—can be added for additional visual interest.

One of the advantages of composite boards is that manufacturers can custom shape the boards to suit the designer's needs. As this photo shows, an elegant curve can be easily added to the deck surface. You can also see the color, grain and texture of the composite boards, often fabricated to mimic the surface of wood.

Composite decking is installed in much the same way as other decking is, although composite decks often use hidden fasteners to avoid telltale lines of screw or nail heads at the end of each board. But where invisible fasteners aren't used, manufacturers supply special screws with heads colored to match the decking you're using, and they blend right in with the surface.

Pie-wedge platforms are a smoother transition down a slope than a set of stairs. The complementary colors composite manufacturers offer make it easy to mix and match as necessary. Here, darker boards give definition to the step-down, in addition to crisply defining the dimensions of the deck. It would have been far more work to use two different colors if the deck had been made of wood.

Aluminum

Elevated decks provide lovely outdoor dining opportunities. Lightweight aluminum decking made this simple deck quicker, easier, and less expensive to build than it would have been using another decking material. It's also a fire-resistant option that won't warp, bow, or split. Not to mention, the colors perfectly complement the color of the home's siding.

A southerly exposure yields plenty of sun, but little sun damage to this aluminum deck. The coating used not only comes in a variety of colors as well as wood-grained tints, it is also fade resistant and slip resistant. Aluminum decks do need structural support, however, which in this case is pressure-treated wood that can be seen in between the tread risers.

It's always a good idea to match your decking material to your location. An aluminum deck was a good choice for this lakefront home. The decking is water- (even salt water) and mold-resistant, and won't rot or rust. The railings are also aluminum, and the homeowner has chosen an elegant color combination of charcoal-gray decking with bright white railings.

Aluminum can be the ideal choice for a modest size ground-level deck. Here, the color and simple shape were chosen to blend in seamlessly with the house and create what is essentially a room without walls. The low-lying structure required modest reinforcement and rot is not a worry with the aluminum decking. Notice how the homeowner used a rock border in a similar shade to the deck to create a harmonious visual link between house and yard.

Deck Tiles

Deck tiles are a quick, simple and inexpensive option to a full-scale deck. Although limited to ground level surfaces—or preexisting, flat, level, and stable surfaces such as balconies—a tile deck can be customized to just about any linear shape. The homeowner created this simple backyard space with staggered corners to add visual interest.

As shown here, deck tiles make for a perfect secluded garden platform detached from the house. An attractive aspect of using deck tiles is the ability to play around with patterns. Here, the deck features simple slatted tiles run in the same direction, with special patterned tiles run in rows. The variation creates a lot of interest underfoot, and the possibilities for different patterns—from herringbone to entirely unique creations—are almost limitless.

Decking tiles are usually produced and sold as square-foot units. Manufacturers offer a selection of hardwoods and composite tiles, and the tiles are produced in simple slatted designs, as shown here, diagonal designs for herringbone patterns, and other board patterns within the single tile. The tiles are normally sold prefinished, requiring only installation

Deck tiles are particularly well suited to cover preexisting hard surfaces, such as the unsightly aging cement pool deck around this pool. The tiles provide an added benefit with their open construction that leaves plenty of room for water to drain away—including around the plastic base—ensuring that the wood does not rot or mold, and keeping the surface from becoming too slick. Notice the reducer tiles used around the edge of the pool, creating the look of a custom deck.

Deck tiles are usually constructed with a plastic base that allows for water drainage and holds the decking material up off the ground. Although connection systems vary from manufacturer to manufacturer, a common method of attachment is plastic tabs that slot into openings on adjacent tiles. This system makes installation extremely easy, requiring no tools in most cases.

Manufacturers produce variations on the basic deck tile to serve in different situations. The side view here is of a "reducer" tile that adds a sloping edge to the border of a deck or over a swimming pool lip. You'll also find special tiles for corners as well as other applications.

Ideal Deck Size and Shape

Deck size and shape are the starting points for your deck's design. That's because deck configuration, and how big or small the structure is, affects how well it serves your needs and fits in with your house and yard. Get the proportions right and the deck will look like it's always been there, and will accommodate whatever uses you have in mind for the space.

Deck size will be constrained to some extent by budget. Other practical concerns will play a part as well. Large landscape features such as old-growth trees may limit how big the deck can be, as will impediments such as severe slopes. Those features will also determine the shape of your deck. Customizing your deck to fit around features in the landscape is a way to make the surface seem a more natural transition between house and yard. But of course, deck shape may also be dictated by other concerns.

Basic squares or rectangles are the easiest—and least expensive—shapes to create. Introduce curves into your deck design and you add visual interest. But severe curves can limit usable space; gentle curves create a more elegant contour. Curves and straight lines are not however, the only shapes available in deck design. You can choose to design a completely unique shape with unusual angles and polygons to define different areas of the deck. Deck shapes are really only limited by imagination. Keep in mind, though, that the shape and size of your deck should always be the servant to the way you will use it. No deck design should emphasize look at the cost of function.

Some locations are more obvious candidates for a deck than others. But this entryway is well served by a tiny deck that is part of a sophisticated entrance design. The curved shape is inviting and space-efficient, directing visitors up the stairs, over the rock moat, and right to the door. The dark color of the ipé decking reinforces the visual sense of a small, intimate landing space in front of the door.

Deck shape and size can help set the mood of an outdoor space, as this simple, square deck does, set into the inside corner of a house. The modest deck complements the restrained dimensions of the space, and the offset step creates visual interest. Stepping stones, a linear border and Japanese-influenced privacy fence all reinforce the notion of a peaceful Zen garden, with the gray composite deck functioning as a meditative platform.

Small doesn't need to equal dull. This deck nestled into the corner of the house features a three-tone color scheme and superb detailing that includes enclosed skirting, which combine to make the deck feel like it is an integral part of the sophisticated architecture. But the landscaping is what provides a finished look to the installation. Foundation plantings and groomed beds help make a small deck blend seamlessly with the house at large.

Long narrow decks are sometimes the best match for conventional settings and traditional architecture. This skinny deck provides a porch-like accent to the house, and mirrors the overall shape of the yard. The deck is meant solely as a sunbathing retreat, one intended to blend in rather than stand out. The color of the composite decking helps this purpose, almost perfectly matching the siding.

Constructed alongside a traditional covered porch, this interestingly shaped deck serves as an ideal viewing platform from which to enjoy a sunny day and the well-landscaped yard. Railing and stair lights also make it a nice place to spend time outside at night stargazing or just enjoying a warm summer's evening.

Just because a deck is small doesn't mean it can't be interesting or special. This tiny outdoor dining area is just large enough to accommodate a small table and chairs for warm-weather cookouts. The money saved from building such a modest deck allowed for details not found on many smaller decks. A built-in bench adds seating and style, and built-in planters add beautiful accents.

Small does not need to equal plain. This tiny deck was built using stunning ipé hardwood in deep reddish browns. But as lovely as the wood itself is, the details are incredibly impressive. Built-in benches and planters ensure this is one very comfortable outdoor room, and the elaborate designs in the railings and overhang supports add to the feeling of a comfortable, cozy space, perfect for reading the paper or having a drink with a few close friends.

Where space is constrained, go vertical. Positioned as a dual level transition into a tiny backyard, this composite deck provides an intimate sitting area on top, linked by stairs to a larger lower deck that can be used for dining, parties, or sunbathing. The entire footprint of the structure takes up a minimum of space.

This deck would have been fairly uninteresting as a rectangle, but a chic curving front surface brings to mind the contour of a grand piano. The shape blends the edge of the deck nicely with the yard's profuse flowering shrubs. The inlaid compass star completes a deck design that while simple, is incredibly stylish.

Crafted of composite decking, this outdoor living room is stylized with a diamond inlay in contrasting color and four different board directions that make for a fascinating surface pattern. But the scalloped shape and a bump-out alcove containing a luxurious spa tub make the look. Bright white trim ties the different areas together and gives the deck a crisp appearance.

Sometimes simple is the order of the day. This composite front deck was meant as a very basic platform overlooking a stunning naturalistic setting. The gray color and simple rectangular shape complement the shape and shades of the landmark stone house. When the architecture is distinctive, it's a good idea to let it dictate the shape of the deck.

The danger in designing a long rectangular deck is that it will become an uninviting, unusable bowling alley. The builder of this deck avoided that fate by creating a bump-out that serves as a comfortable alcove for seating and creates a more dynamic shape for the deck. Making the deck even more unusual, the long inner side has been left unattached to the house, with a bench serving as both railing and additional seating.

Create a very pleasing look in a large deck by using symmetry to provide visual balance. This attractive deck includes matching border benches on either side that not only offer abundant seating, they also help focus the eye and lead the visitor to the stone path running out into the backyard garden. The homeowner has carried through the idea of symmetry with planters on either side the sliding glass doors.

Large deck design is almost always successful when the style of the structure matches the style of the home. Here, a large, multilevel deck echoes the conservative and traditional lines of the house itself, and the deck has been crafted in a monochromatic composite material that draws its color cues from the bright white trim of the house. Consequently, house and deck seem all of a piece.

Keep a large deck in perspective to the home and yard by using different shapes throughout the structure. The deck shown here is a good example of how to create what visually reads as different decks by using an octagonal platform overlooking a pool, situated opposite the dining portion of the deck. White railings and a white arbor unify the variations in shape and tie the whole deck to the house.

Where space is not an issue—as in this acre-size backyard—you can be extravagant with the deck design. This deck features several outdoor "rooms," with a large spa tub, a separate fireplace seating area, and cooking and dining sections. The abundance of space allows each area enough separation to stand on its own, with the deck surface tying all of them together.

COMPUTER-AIDED DECK DESIGN

Looking for a dynamite deck design? Put down your sketchpad and pencil, and turn to the computer. You can find a wealth of computer-aided design (CAD) programs specifically created to help the homeowner design the ideal deck. Derived from powerful, complex CAD software used by professionals such as architects, the deck design programs available today are user-friendly, adaptable, and incredibly helpful. Most people will be able to master any of these programs within a couple hours. The software allows you to create a representation of your home, design the deck to highly detailed specifications, and see your creation in a color, three-dimensional model. Although you are likely find the ability to preview potential designs one of the most attractive features, these programs also provide other useful functions, such as materials calculators, the ability to swap elements with a few clicks of the mouse, and ways to keep track of costs once you start your project.

Many deck design programs allow you to create plan views—elevation drawings detailed enough to be accepted by some building departments as part of the permit process. These elevation plans can be extremely helpful if you are hiring a contractor or deck builder to construct the deck for you.

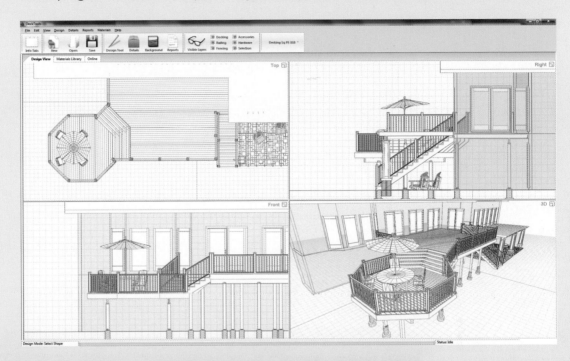

This screen capture is representative of the level of detail you can expect from most deck-design programs. The software creates scale models of the deck you've designed, and many programs allow you to view the deck from multiple angles. You can also change the color of the deck to see how it would look crafted from different decking materials.

Deck Perspectives

Every deck must take into account several different points of view. The most obvious is the perspective from the deck looking out into the yard and surroundings. But the deck also changes the view from inside the house, altering the perspective the homeowner sees as he or she looks out a window or through glass doors. No less important, the deck will greatly affect the appearance of the house.

All of these are most affected by the level of the deck. A ground-level platform is less likely to dramatically change the view from inside the house, and it will usually only have a modest impact on how the house's architecture is perceived. A multilevel or elevated deck will provide a much greater vista of the yard and beyond, while also radically changing how the architecture is perceived. Obviously, how you site your deck is an extremely important part of your design.

But beyond view and appearances, the levels of your deck are also a structural concern. It will always be easier to build a deck at ground level on a nice, flat, level plot. The higher and more complicated the deck is, the greater the engineering must be to ensure that it is safe. Structural reinforcement also adds to the cost of the project. That's why, ultimately, the final perspective of any deck design is a balance between the look—or looks—you desire and the more fundamental, practical concerns of construction.

A ground-level deck need not be a boring, one-dimensional platform. Although this deck is built at ground level, it includes a step-up level of its own, providing variation and a seating area separate from the main stage of the deck. Bushy flowering perennials and low-growing evergreen shrubs help blend the structure into the surrounding yard.

Help a ground-level deck look as crisp as possible by using fascia boards around the perimeter. The fascia on this deck matches the composite decking material used on top—replicating the coloring and patterns of ipé hardwood. Matching fascia boards create the illusion of a solid box set level on the ground. Separate dining, fire pit, and spa tub areas are defined simply by furniture placement, rather than separate platform levels.

The simplest decks are those without foundations. Done right, as in the case of this small backyard deck, even a tiny deck can bring big impact to the yard and house. The designer of this composite deck chose a bold treatment, with a darker color border, decking installed on a diagonal, and a bridge that crosses a pond of rocks. The effect is far more eye-catching than the square footage would suggest.

A small side yard deck provides a lovely step-out fresh-air dining room. By building a thicker platform that raises the deck surface to the level of the door threshold, the homeowner created a more fluid transition from inside to out, and one that makes carrying plates of food for grilling outside much easier. Subtle steps cut into one corner of the thick platform provide stylish access to the backyard.

Deck design should always answer the owner's needs first. This composite ground-level deck was designed and built to blend in seamlessly without calling much attention to itself. The solid-color deck material seems almost like an extension of the house's painted walls, and the triple steps leading from twin sets of sliding glass doors make a seamless visual connection from inside to out.

A stunning hardwood deck is made even more so designed with an unusual, long angular shape the builder positioned across the corner of the house. Rather than raise the deck to the house level, the builder used a set of steps to a transition platform at the back door. The deck is integrated with the yard through strategically placed plantings, and a bit of flair is added with a wing-shaped shade sail over the sitting area.

Small is sometimes the best size for a given location. This gently curved front entryway deck provides much of the charm of a porch, without overwhelming the front yard or walk leading up to the door. By elevating the deck, the designer makes it seem like an attractive, inviting extension of the entryway threshold.

Making an elevated deck with visible supports stylish, means paying attention to the details. The support members holding up this large deck have been clad in the same material as the deck. Rather than leave the underdeck area an unappealing dirt surface, the builder laid a cement border and filled in with decorative rock—a great way to turn an eyesore area into a more attractive element.

View and sun exposure are two big benefits of an elevated deck; this second-floor cedar deck enjoys both. A bright white aluminum railing adds style. The deck doubles as a sunbathing platform during the day, and a social center any time. The structure was positioned to take advantage of a scenic stand of trees surrounding the yard, which would have bathed a lower deck in shade.

An elevated deck can be the perfect solution to a sloped site. This house featured a grass-covered backyard that was pleasant to look at, but too steep to use for summer cookouts or entertaining. The second-floor deck serves those purposes nicely and provides an excellent vantage point for looking out over the peaceful view. The supports for the deck were left exposed because they'll rarely be viewed from the seldom-used yard.

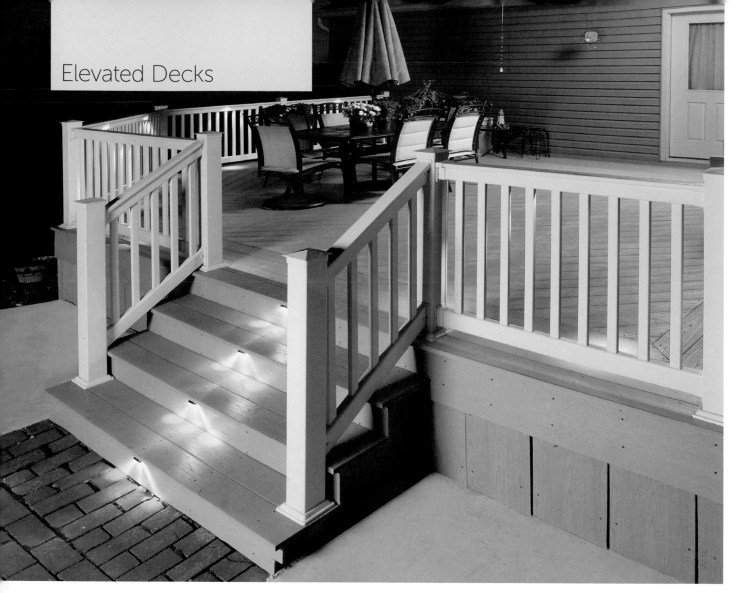

There are many ways to deal with the less-than-attractive supporting framework that holds up elevated decks. The solution here is one of the best: cladding the outside of the foundation with a skirting of the same material as the decking. The wide composite fascia and skirting used on this deck matches the decking and stairs, creating a unified design that makes for an attractive platform, especially when lit at night.

A pleasing deck design can be understated rather than flashy. The subtle design of this all-brown deck incorporates some basic and inexpensive style features, like decking run on the diagonal in sections, and a cantilevered construction that hides supporting members in shadow. The subdued nature of this outdoor cookout platform is entirely appropriate against the neutral clapboard siding and evergreen backyard.

Another way to hide an elevated deck's supporting structure is with wraparound stairs. The stairs on this simple deck are crafted of the same wood as the decking, which makes the entire structure visually read like one solid piece. Wraparound stairs are a lot of work to design and install, but the final appearance is usually well worth the effort.

A curved facade can be a powerful design element for an elevated deck. This hardwood deck emphasizes the prow of the structure with a contrasting white fascia that makes the deck visually project out even more. Decorative railings and lattice between stained supports below the deck create an interesting and sophisticated look.

An elegant, two-tiered ipé hardwood deck provides clearly separate areas for enjoying an outdoor meal and relaxing in front of a simple fire pit. Separating areas of a deck with different levels not only defines the function of those different spaces, it also adds an interesting visual change along the deck's surface. The designer of this deck added to the appeal by orienting it at two different angles to the house.

Variation can be the spice of deck design, as this structure shows. A "spillover" deck was added to the main deck to provide extra space during parties and large family get-togethers. The small deck has been designed as an auxiliary, purposely different in the lack of railings and the presence of a built-in bench. The common composite decking material ties the platforms together.

Large decks offer the opportunity to incorporate large style. This fabulous deck features cascading levels that flow into one another by way of elegantly curved steps. Built-in planters help define the different levels, and a spa tub serves as a visual centerpiece of the two-tone composite surface. A large inlaid compass rose adds even more polish to an already highly sophisticated look.

The choice of all white decking and railings gives this bilevel structure a very clean look. Even the enclosed pergola roof is white. Cladding a pergola in a solid surface helps block the direct sun for cool meals on hot days, and means the space can be used even in inclement weather. Post-cap lights are as practical as they are pretty, making the deck usable at night as well as day.

Decks in the Landscape

The best decks just look like they belong. They seem right in proportion to the house, and they complement rather than compete with the landscape. One of the best ways to make your deck look like it's always been there is by creating tangible connections between the structure itself and your landscape.

That isn't really hard to do, if you consider the layout of your yard when designing your deck. A strong link between the structure you build and the property you own can actually be established in a number of different ways—or a combination of them. You can, for example, shape a deck to conform to hallmark features in the landscape. Many deck designers do this by including access holes for beautiful old trees to grow right through the surface of the deck. You can also carry through the theme of a garden or landscape by decorating the deck with planters potted with similar plants. Of course, a natural way to integrate the deck into a yard is to landscape around the structure once you've completed it.

Whatever technique you use, always keep in mind the view from the deck—yet another excellent way to reinforce the connection with natural surroundings. Position your deck to look over foliage and flowers from three sides, and you create an immediate link to that vegetation. A scene thick with plant life creates a wonderful mood, conducive to relaxation, easy socializing and, ultimately, complete enjoyment of the space. Successfully make the connection between nature and your deck and you'll create a structure that not only serves as a perfect transition from inside to out, but one that improves both yard and garden.

Overgrowth can be the deck designer's best friend. As this deck illustrates, positioning the deck so that flowering and evergreen shrubs invade the borders of the deck is a great way to blur the distinction between deck and garden. This composite surface seems to disappear into plant life on every side, not only blending the deck, but also creating an idealic environment for relaxing or eating outside.

The lower the deck, the easier it is to blend the structure into the landscape. This ipé deck seems to meld into its naturalistic surroundings. The homeowner has run the mulched beds around the border under the actual deck, blurring boundaries. A mix of planted and potted plants reinforces the union between structure and landscape, with vegetation growing right up against the edges of the deck.

A deck's surrounding landscape is sometimes not land. Connected to the shore by a peninsula, this wood deck is actually immersed in its environment. It's meant specifically for the owners of this lakefront property to soak up the sun and enjoy the watery surroundings. Unconventional decks in unusual places can be some of the most special platforms.

The creative design of this deck ensures that the structure is one with the beautifully landscaped yard. The deck actually serves as both a relaxing platform and a pathway from house to pool. The levels of the deck follow the contours of the yard, and run it right through informal plantings. The placement means that sunbathers relax in the midst of the landscape.

Although most decks are designed to conform to the landscape, you can also landscape to complement the design of the deck. This homeowner created a garden bed under the deck's wood staircase. The color and form of the ornamental grasses and informal scattering of low-growing shrubs perfectly complement the rustic look of the wood rails and stairs. The result is a staircase that visually roots the deck into the landscape.

The easiest way to merge a deck with the landscape is to design it to hug the topography. This is an especially effective strategy when dealing with multiple levels, as with this deck. This deck was designed to almost organically nestle into the hillside. effectively making it look like it has been there forever and is just an extension of the landscape. The use of redwood for the decking increases this perception, because the color of the wood blends so well with plants and soil.

Decks can be a wonderful way to extend the home into dense natural surroundings. This expansive deck was designed with a seemingly random outdoor border that follows the contours of the wooded hillside behind the house. The deck has been built with an opening to allow a tree to grow through the surface, and further tie the outdoor space to the surrounding environment.

If you're fortunate enough to live in a woodsy setting, you should make the most of it with any deck you build. This simple wood platform was built on a large wooded property, but rather than cut down trees to make room for the deck, the deck was designed to jut out into a copse of trees. The tree canopies hang over the deck, creating a bucolic feel.

This simple ground-level deck was built to bump right up against the evergreens, trees, and foliage plants scattered throughout the informal landscaping of the yard. Plants grow over the edge of the deck, and a tree branch even grows under the arbor, creating a backyard spa tub experience that is more like a luxurious getaway in a tropical location.

A stunning mountainside deck benefits from a unique design that makes room for a tree, with a "tree ring" built into the deck's surface. Tree rings are simple elements of the construction for experienced deck builders and are a way for the deck to coexist with wonderful old-growth trees. This homeowner went one step further and added a self-contained deck-top garden with a plastic liner and rock walls.

Focus on Purpose

You can build the most beautiful deck in the world, but if it doesn't serve the purpose you want it to, you'll use it less than you otherwise would. Ultimately, it won't be the life-enhancing outdoor addition a deck truly should be. In fact, a deck that doesn't suit the purpose the homeowner intended for it is a huge waste of time and money.

That's why any successful deck design must take into account the ways in which the homeowner wants to use the surface and the space. After all, accommodating a spa tub requires a different structure and layout than creating an inviting sitting area to enjoy a stunning, wraparound view. Just building a platform in the backyard won't get you very far.

Of course, this means you have to have a clear idea of how you want to use the deck before you start planning the design. There are many, many options. Decks are perfect as luxurious spa-tub platforms and supporting players to a built-in pool. But they can also serve as outdoor kitchens and dining rooms for memorable al fresco meals. A deck can be designed for large cocktail parties or for small, intimate gatherings of friends. It can be the lookout platform that takes advantage of stunning views, or it can simply be a sun worshiper's stage for regular tanning sessions. Whatever you intend to do on your deck, make sure that the purpose drives the design, and you'll be taking a big step toward building a structure that is as enjoyable and usable as possible.

Spa tubs are perfect for isolated decks away from a main house and out of the neighbor's view. This tree-shrouded location lends privacy to the spa-tub experience, and the hardwood decking adds elegance as well as an easy step-up design. Consider how shy you are about being seen in a bathing suit before you decide on how much—or little—privacy you want in your spa-tub deck location.

The spa-tub experience lends itself to a tropical setting. The owner of this deck and tub has nestled the feature into a landscape that might be an island paradise. The slat decking and low railing provide an understated foil that allows the tub and surroundings to dominate the scene. A tub-side ledge adds a little useful luxury to the picture, providing a handy place for drinks and food.

A spa tub is the ideal centerpiece for any deck. Here, the round deck is meant merely as a stage for the tub, isolated in the center of the patio. When planning a tub deck location, keep the view in mind as the owner of this tub did; the tub's positioning takes advantage of the rural setting's wonderful 360-degree view. Because no neighbors are within site, privacy was not an issue.

Most spa tubs are clad in a wood or faux wood to blend in with the deck surface. But this particular model features a faux-stone surround that helps the tub stand out. The tub was added after the deck was built, but the crossing deck board pattern was specifically designed to frame a tub. Decking direction is a great way to draw attention to any feature on the deck.

A pergola and matching privacy screen help define and separate the spa tub area of this large deck. Privacy screens are elegant ways to create intimate spaces for tubbing out of view of neighbors or even other people in the house. The pergola breaks up direct sun, but still allows a view of the stars for nights in the tub.

The right deck can create a little spa heaven, private and inviting. The deck here was crafted of tigerwood that is, like other hardwoods, resistant to mold, water damage, cracking, and slipping. The appearance of the deck is stunning, but no less so at night, when the tub's lavender lights illuminate the heated water to create a nearly surreal vision of relaxation. Consider colored lighting to spruce up the look of a basic tub or pool.

A compact, well-designed deck allows for a single purpose to dominate, without the feature completely overwhelming the look of the deck itself. These homeowners use their spa tub as the centerpiece of outdoor parties. The deck layout facilitates easy access to the spa tub itself, and keeps adjacent seating close enough for bathers and non-bathers to pleasantly interact. The deck's clear, heart-grade redwood has been water-sealed, but is naturally resistant to rot, wear, and cracking.

When purchasing your spa tub, consider accents that will increase your enjoyment of the luxury. Here, the owner has opted to supplement the tub with steps, planters and bleacher seating all supplied by the tub's manufacturer. Notice that the tub's surround matches the composite decking. Many manufacturers offer your choice of tub surrounds to help the feature blend in with the decking you've selected.

Multilevel decks are well-suited for a spa tub. This hillside deck incorporates the tub into the second of three levels. The design makes both a natural progression on the steep slope, and separates the tub into its own space. Notice that the tub is accompanied by a built-in bench; built-in seating gives bathers a place to cool off or change into and out of bathing gear.

Pool Fun

An in-ground swimming pool is the height of luxury. So it stands to reason, an equally luxurious decking material is called for. This inviting oval pool is well-served with handsome cumaru hardwood decking. One of the densest hardwoods used for decking, cumaru is naturally resistant to insects, mold, rot, and water penetration. Installed around a pool, only the cut ends need to be water-sealed.

This stunning composite deck blends perfectly into the surroundings. It also complements the pool, letting the stone-bordered body of water bask in the attention it deserves. The high-quality composite material won't rot, warp, or be adversely affected by water from the pool. The railings and deck are made from the same material, and the color was chosen specifically to meld with the natural colors surrounding the hillside home.

A deck that contrasts the pool area can be as powerful as one that complements it. The deck shown here leads from the main floor of the house, down to a pool bordered with a concrete patio. The darkness of the hardwood cumaru decking stands out against the light surfaces and water of the pool. It provides a transition from beige house siding to pool area, one that includes seating overlooking the pool.

Decks don't have to dominate poolside to be a wonderful addition to the setting. This small hardwood platform provides a relaxing respite from the hard (and sometimes sun-hot) surface of the brick patio. It provides an interesting variation in pattern and texture, and is tied to the rest of the pool's surface with brick pylons that hold up a wood arbor.

Simplicity is sometimes the essence of elegance when it comes to designing a pool deck. Although this deck doesn't shout with color or pattern, the beige composite material creates a sophisticated look with a surface that is water-and wear-resistant. The designer crafted a stylish lip by running the decking over the edge of the pool and cladding it with a fascia board. The effect is sleek, modern, and pleasing to the eye.

This elegant gray composite deck complements both the house's siding and the pool's white concrete lip. The shape of the deck roughly echoes the shape of the pool, but with intriguing variations and bump-outs around the perimeter. Note how the direction of the boards around the outside of the pool form a separate border. Board direction is a great way to create this kind of emphasis on a signature feature.

Pool decks can function as a design bridge.
They are great for couching the pool in the style and context of the house—especially when the house features distinctive architecture. This modern home is complemented by a simple weathered redwood pool deck that echoes the basic straight lines of the architecture, with boards running perpendicular to the length of the pool. It's a simple and graceful look that serves the purpose—a comfortable surface underfoot—admirably.

A pool deck doesn't necessarily have to be attached to the pool. The deck here is separated from the pool by a paver patio, but it still provides a shaded overhang—an ideal spot for swimmers to take a cooling time-out from playing in the pool. A privacy fence alongside the deck allows for dining in swimsuits without being self-conscious.

A well-designed pool deck should frame the pool and leave abundant room for people to not only get in and out, but socialize as well (pools are inevitably the center of parties). This large deck answers the call on both points. Although it is largely functional, the owner has added a bit of style by using wood handrails finished in a natural tone that pops against the gray of the deck.

Elevated decks are ideal for poolside placement. They provide a vantage point for parents to supervise youngsters playing in the pool, and increase visual interest from the pool. This deck brings some stylistic fireworks in the form of stone posts that work well with the tan decking and skirting. The posts add a stately element to both deck and pool, enriching the entire scene.

Pool Fun

Decks built around a yard feature are often most effective and attractive when they follow the contours of that feature. This is especially true with swimming pools. This kidney-shaped pool might have looked odd surrounded by a deck in a geometric shape. But the curving deck here suits the pool well, with a row of potted plants to blur the boundary between weathered deck boards and the concrete pool edging.

When it comes to pool decks, only one or the other should grab the attention. This wonderful redwood deck positions the pool as centerpiece, but it's the wood's distinctive color and grain that really tease the eye. A bump-out covered by a large pergola provides broken shade for swimmers who want to cool off, and a rail of the same wood provides a safety barrier required by most codes.

A pool deck need not surround the pool to be of use or to create a lovely accent. Here, a simple deck provides a variation in surfaces off to one side of the pool. It's a solid surface where the sun can be enjoyed out of the water, but one that won't get hot underfoot. A basic privacy fence blocks the neighbors' view, creating a perfect secluded spot for intimate relaxation.

Aboveground pools can be a bit unsightly when sticking up in the middle of the backyard. An elevated deck that butts up to the edge of the pool improves the look of the pool and the yard by large measure. The platform also provides much more convenient access to the pool than a basic ladder would.

When you have a spectacular view, design your deck to take advantage of it. This deck does just that, with a curving front edge like the prow of a ship. It projects out into the view, bringing the forested hillside almost within touching distance. The owner has provided two seating areas, one shaded and the other open to the sun. But thanks to the deck design, both enjoy a panoramic view of nature that is simply unrivaled.

Even a modest backyard deck can be a lovely place to take in nature's show. Running along the back of the house, this deck is elevated in respect to the sloped and wooded backyard. The owners have furnished it with comfortable Adirondack chairs and use it to watch birds, and generally decompress among the wealth of plant life.

An upstairs deck punctuated with thick beams that support an A-frame overhang is the ideal place to see the trees beyond in all their glory. Tempered glass panels in the handrails ensure that as much of the view can be seen as possible. The benefit of a deck positioned as high as this one is that at night, the stars provide yet another reason to spend time gazing out at the horizon.

Consider lighting and the nighttime deck when designing for view. The deck after dark often provides a wholly different visual feast, sometimes even more intriguing than what you would see during the day. This multilevel deck has been lit with restraint, allowing hypnotic shadows to dominate the night landscape and barely illuminate the surface of the pool. The captivating scene is as nice a view as you'll find on any deck, day or night.

Waterfront exposures scream for a deck that takes advantage of them. This structure was built almost to the river's edge, but high enough to ensure that even in the rainy season, the deck will be above the water. The peaceful picture created by the water and the hills in the distance draws attention at all hours.

Decks play well in a landscape dominated by a diversity of trees, shrubs, and other plant life. This large yard is filled with a dense, forested landscape, one that provides almost endless fascination to anyone seated on the deck. Different levels on the deck provide different vantage points and different views, making the surroundings even more interesting.

Second-story decks are natural vantage points. If your home can accommodate one, they can be perfect for enjoying a gardener's gem or a well-landscaped yard. This deck was designed to look out over a professionally cultivated property, complete with rock garden and reflecting pool. The cabled handrails allow maximum view over the yard, and add big flair to the entire structure.

Siting a deck to take advantage of a beautiful view is never a bad idea, even if the initial intention is not necessarily to use the deck as a viewing platform. These homeowners chose to locate their deck on a corner overlooking their tree-studded backyard. Although they've created a conversation nook with a cluster of chairs and tables, the view is always there as a fabulous backdrop. A great view will never go to waste.

Views seen from below can be as powerful as views seen from above, as this deck proves. Physical beauty rises up on all sides of this multi-level deck, with intensely landscaped scenery filling the field of view no matter where a visitor to the deck might look. The flowering hillsides compete for attention with the pool, but the winner is anyone enjoying the show from a chair on the deck.

Evergreens surround this house in the country, providing a serene and bucolic view from every angle. The deck designer took the opportunity to create multiple perspectives. The hot tub looks out over a patch of grass, while the dining table enjoys an entirely different view of trees. Creating multiple perspectives is a way to add even more visual interest to a deck that is already ripe with it.

For devoted foodies, chefs, and big eaters alike, there's no outdoor space quite like an outdoor kitchen and dining deck. Although a fully functional outdoor kitchen requires much more planning than other types of decks—including running wiring and possibly other utilities—the return on investment can be huge. A well-equipped kitchen such as this one, with range and refrigerator, can make the deck even more enjoyable and usable. In temperate parts of the country, functional outdoor spaces like this will see use nearly year-round.

Covering the outdoor kitchen portion of the deck makes preparing meals more comfortable for this homeowner. It also defines the cooking area, setting it apart from lower dining level. The deck builder has set aside abundant room for food preparation, and to allow more than one person to work in the outdoor kitchen at a time.

Meals are a pleasure to prepare in this elegant outdoor cook's space. Outfitted with cooktop, sink, prep area, and just about anything a cook might need, the kitchen is also comfortable thanks to a two-tier pergola overhang that provides broken shade. The wood decking has been finished to repel any stains—a necessary step if you truly intend to use an outdoor kitchen to its full potential.

This interesting deck was designed as a series of intersecting angles. The unique layout makes clear separations between individual areas, including a spa tub alcove, a dining room, a conversation pit, and a cooking area. Clearly defining different areas of a multiuse deck is key to making it enjoyable and useful for everyone.

Using one feature as the focal point of your deck is a great way to gain separation between different areas of a multipurpose deck. This is particularly effective with single-level decks, such as the one shown here. The centerpiece makes for a natural positioning of the other areas, and draws attention to the feature or purpose you intend to use the most.

When different areas of the deck are in close quarters, create separation with design and construction elements. This deck was built with a step-up level for the dining and seating area, to separate it from the spa tub. The composite decking includes a different color border to increase the sense of separation between areas.

If you have plenty of space and a deep pocketbook, the sky is the limit to the number of uses to which you can put your deck. This multifunctional platform includes integrated—rather than clearly separated—areas. The hot tub shares space with the fire pit (a natural marriage) and seating areas are clustered around a bar and outdoor kitchen, making the transition from one area to another very fluid.

Deck Features

Just like clothes make the man, design details make the deck. Although there's no crime in building a simple, plain platform to take advantage of a backyard view, or as a no-frills summer hangout to share a few drinks with friends, it's the very rare deck that isn't improved with one or more built-in features.

Some of these are required. Handrails, for instance, are mandated by local codes for decks a certain height above the ground. Stairs are simply practical necessities for elevated or multilevel decks. As practical as these features may be, however, they can also be built with incredible style.

Other deck additions serve specific needs. Light fixtures, a privacy fence, or a pergola that breaks up the direct sun exposure over a spa tub will make your deck much more comfortable. Some features bridge that line between function and looks. Benches are a prime example. Although they supply a practical place to sit down, they are not, strictly speaking, necessary.

Other features are more—or completely—aesthetic in nature. A planter or a fire pit makes a deck more enchanting and makes the time you spend there more pleasant. Inlaid designs gracing the surface of a deck are likewise simple decorations. But when you're dealing with what can be such a plain feature in the yard, these types of treatments can have tremendous impact.

That's why no matter what built-in feature you're considering for your deck design, always keep appearances in mind. No feature on a deck should look like an afterthought. As much as a wonderful latticework fence can add to a deck, a poorly designed, tacked-on bench or overhang will surely detract from it.

Steep staircases can seem daunting and unbalancing. That is why the designer of this composite deck interrupted the staircase with a landing halfway down the run. Landings add a more inviting perspective to the deck, and make it much more comfortable to climb the stairs. Wraparound stairs, such as these, make the deck more accessible, as well.

Contrast is one of the most powerful ways to make deck railings stand out. The black of these metal balusters, post caps, and rail hangers all pop against the tan of the composite decking. The railing gets a splash of added flair with the scrollworked baluster accents. Because it is so apparent, this type of detail carries a lot of weight in how the overall deck will be perceived.

A wonderful thing about working with iron is its malleability. These balusters have been bent to a distinctive shape, one that draws the eye along the railing. Notice that the designer used balusters of the same shape; varying the shapes would have created visual chaos. The builder also paid attention to the fine details, such as attaching the balusters with screws that had blackened heads—successfully avoiding eyesores that might mar the look.

A sure way to bring a deck railing to life is to go vivid. The clean white and sharp black of this railing pop out against the tan of the deck. The deck, rails and posts are all composite materials, which translates to a lower cost of fabrication than if the railings were constructed of hardwood. It also means the railings will look sharp for years to come with minimal maintenance.

Iron, metal, and aluminum balusters come in a variety of specialized designs, including the twisting spirals shown here. Choose the number of decorative balusters you include in each section of rail to make your deck borders unique. Of course, if you're willing to go to the extra expense, you can have metal balusters bent to custom designs by a metal shop.

There are few better ways to dress up plain wood railings than with decorative wrought-iron balusters. The unadorned lines of this staircase serve as foil for the wavy contours of the iron balusters. The wood's dull brown surface is more attractive when played against the metal's gloss black finish. Not only is the look much sharper than all-wood pieces would have been, the rail-attached balusters are simple to install.

Where pool decks are concerned, railings are as much a safety feature as an aesthetic addition. The railing here keeps children on the deck, while looking great with post-cap lights in the color of the balusters, and decorative baluster accents. But the most important feature of this particular railing is the safety gate that has been crafted to blend in with the railings themselves, while keeping small children away from the pool.

Mounting railing on the fascia is a sleek look that frees up deck space. As shown here, this mounting style is sleek and maximizes the usable area of the deck. But be sure to check and follow local codes—the posts must be mounted in a secure fashion to prevent accidents.

Wood-and-iron railings are a traditional deck treatment and one that has stood the test of time. The evenly spaced tube balusters shown here are understated, and the black powder coating is not only resistant to the elements, it is also a perfect complement to the dark wood railing. The look is finished with post-mounted downlights and rail hangers in the same finish as the balusters.

Aluminum is a good option for durable, attractive railings. Aluminum balusters come in a variety of stylish shapes and configurations. The classic black-and-tan finish on this railing is powder coated to hold up against years of weather, sun, and deck use. Aluminum railings also come with the same accessories featured on composite and wood railings. This particular construction incorporates stunning post-cap lights that add panache as well as illumination.

Unusual combinations of materials can be as stunning in a railing as they can be in a deck. This handcrafted wood railing features old-world touches that play against the look of high-tech stainless steel tube balusters. It's a highly unusual look, but one that works well. Railings are a great place to try out innovative combinations such as this, because they are so easily changed if the combinations don't work.

Lighting is a tremendous way to dress up the posts in your railings. Today's manufacturers offer a variety of railing lighting fixtures, providing you with exceptional design flexibility. Composite posts, such as the one shown here, are usually constructed hollow or with a channel that allows for hardwired fixtures. This post features a decorative "sleeve" light around the top, and a mounted hood light for lighting up the deck's surface.

Composite railing materials have created the same types of possibilities in railing design as they have in deck design. This composite post features a highly detailed post cap, with rail fasteners that blend in wonderfully, and a composite top-rail fillet in a wood grain and color. The look is tasteful, refined, and easy to create.

Real wood posts offer their own unique design potential. This handcrafted railing borders a lakefront deck, and features a hand-carved dragonfly design in the posts. The pointed top of the post has been capped with a miniature wood roof. These details ensure railing posts are every bit as eye-catching as the view from the deck.

Railings

Railing posts are an excellent place to make a statement on your deck. Stone posts, such as the one shown here, can add a distinguished feel to any railing. As this one shows, stone also blends well with the wood components of a railing. This is actually a prefab stone post, with a sleek wired-in metal light fixture that adds a tiny accent to the look.

Just as curves in a deck design spell elegance, a curving rail is a lovely addition to an arced deck edge. This particular curve is made easier to construct with the use of composite materials. Composite manufacturers can actually extrude the railing in the shape of the curve, leaving only a fairly simple installation. Composite materials present many dynamic railing design opportunities.

When it comes to railing post style, the devil is in the details—and the details make the look. This white composite post was constructed with molding that mimics a millworked footing. Notice that the connection between bottom rail and post is finished with the same treatment, all of which gives the post and railing an incredibly polished appearance.

A craftsman-style railing is both durable and memorable. As this post clearly shows, a handmade railing can include details no pre-fabricated type can match. The builder of this deck included details such as pegged construction, thick rope handrail, millworked post top, and a custom peaked, steel post cap that is the icing on the cake of this spectacular railing design.

Steel cable railings have become a conventional look for contemporary and modern decks. Using exposed "button" fasteners for the cable ends is an easy way to add small splashes of style. As shown on the end post for this beige composite railing, the fasteners can present a different color so that instead of blending with the post—the traditional way of treating hardware—the fasteners stand out.

Exceptional craftsmanship is the hallmark of the finest decks no matter what the material. The post in this stained, hardwood rail has been run up through the top rail fillet—rather than simply attaching the fillets to the side of the post. The post has been topped with a hand-turned finial. The detailing is amazing, and the precision of the construction is sure to draw rave reviews.

Where tempered glass railing inserts are concerned, it's important to present them so that they appear as an integral part of the planned design. The builder of this railing created hardwood edge channels for the inserts to slide into, rather than use easier and more common side fasteners. This treatment makes the inserts look like framed windows, and adds a graceful element to the entire rail design.

A pure white rail is an excellent companion to glass railing inserts. The white creates a clean, bright look. Notice that rather than just suspending the inserts between two posts, the designer used detailed top and bottom rails that capture the glass and yet leave plenty of viewing space for watching the changeable water scene.

This is another way to use transparent railing inserts. Although the most common style is solid inserts, the deck builder here used strips as balusters in this handcrafted wood railing. Juxtaposing materials in a railing in this way can create amazing visual interest. But be careful to maintain balance. In this railing, the wood and its details dominate, with the glass serving as a supporting player.

Railings

The steel cables in a cabled railing are usually so subtle that it makes sense for the railing construction itself to be subdued. The construction of this railing is suitably modest, with a fairly plain top rail and post, and no bottom rail at all. The result is very clean and restrained, a look that would be appropriate on many different styles of decks.

The sleek nature of rail cabling lends itself to dark-stained hardwood posts, such as the ones used on this elevated deck. The combination of the posts' basic forms, a flat, almost featureless top rail, and the cables, creates a very modern look, even though the house itself is not a modern style. Fortunately, the clean, spare lines of cabled railings like this one complement just about any type of architecture.

If your deck is in danger of becoming boring, cabled railings can add a spark to the look. This deck and stairs were designed to blend into the wooded hillside, and the construction is rather plain. But the use of cables in the handrails adds an interesting element. As a bonus, the cables used in different areas catch sun at different times, visually reading as lighter or darker at any given moment.

A mix-and-match approach to railing design can be exciting when it works, as this fascinating deck barrier proves. The cabling is so visually minimal that it doesn't clash with the other elements as standard balusters might have. Use different colors in posts and rails for a dynamic look. This one is accented by black rail hangers and post-mounted lights.

Railings

You don't necessarily need to make a design statement with your railing, especially when the material you're using is already handsome in its own right. This attractive wood railing matches the deck, creating a pleasant visual continuity. The actual design of the railing is fairly simple and straightforward. That means it not only complements the overall look of the structure, it also facilitates ease of construction.

A monochromatic, single-material railing can be just the right thing in the right spot. Here, a white railing seems to pop out of the neutral-toned deck, with a traditional, dignified form that adds some measure of class and style to the deck and the house. But mostly, the standardized form is easy on the eyes, allowing the compelling view from the deck to dominate the scene.

If the deck surface is dramatic, using the same treatment for the railings will only add to the drama. The exceptional hardwood deck shown here was stained dark and finished with a high gloss coating. The same finish was used on the matching railings. The grain patterns and deep color work with fine details such as millworked post caps to create a lasting impression of unrivaled sophistication.

Even pressure-treated pine railings can have their moments. The builder of this deck used an innovative approach, painting the deck and top rail fillet a plum color. He also incorporated a traditional "Chippendale" pattern inside the railing. Regardless of the material you're using for the railing construction, a pattern such as this adds an incredible amount of visual interest.

Some of the best built-in deck seating is nearly invisible, serving as almost an extension of the deck surface. This gray composite deck features a simple block-style L bench in one corner. The positioning is not accidental; by running one leg of the L along a house wall, the bench has a natural back surface against which people can lean, making the bench more comfortable and useful.

When designing a meandering deck shape like this one, it helps to use benches and railings to visually define the borders of the deck. This is especially true where the deck borders will almost fade into naturalistic surroundings. The benches used here, and repeated at opposite corners, are slotted to allow the moisture inherent in the location to pass through without causing mold or rot problems.

If you're going to the expense of built-in seating, look for other functions that can be built-in with it. A perfect example of hybrid function in a built-in feature, this simple bench has an ice cooler incorporated. The high-quality composite used for the deck and bench is resistant to rot, decay, water and insect infiltration, making it an ideal material for the cooler.

The zigzag pattern of these benches makes for a very interesting look as well as being far easier to install than curved or enclosed benches. The slats allow moisture to fall through the seats of the benches, and what remains causes little damage because the benches are made—like the deck below them—of clear heart redwood that is nearly impervious to rot and insect infestation.

Crafted of the alluring hardwood ipé, this built-in bench features a curved shape at once graceful and accommodating. The open-design handrail that serves as backing for the benches maintains visual flow and establishes a very sophisticated style that is right in keeping with the refined appearance of ipé's beautiful color and grain. Details like this evidence the hand of a fine craftsman, and separate basic decks from really special outdoor areas.

Built-in benches can really spruce up a small or plain deck. The edge benches built in to this deck are interspersed with planters, to provide not only abundant seating for parties and gatherings, but to also create a sense of closure and intimacy and add a certain complexity to the deck design. The deck would seem very bare without these built-in features.

This highly detailed deck includes an incredible compass rose in the middle of the deck's surface. If your budget will allow for an expensive accent, an inlay as detailed as this one can be a hallmark feature that serves as a unique work of art. This design was created of the same composite material as the deck, but required a skilled professional with the abilities necessary to make extremely fine cuts.

A spectacular mountain-side vista isn't the only gaze-grabbing feature of this composite deck. The lookout extension designed into the structure features an inlaid compass rose. This is one of the most common designs used for inlays, both because it's a traditional design with storied nautical roots, and it's a simpler shape to actually inlay into the deck than one with many curves or intricate figures.

A deck inlay doesn't necessarily need to be extremely complex. Even a fairly basic design adds variety and draws the eye to the deck's surface. This diamond was executed in a solid color that contrasted the overall decking, but the pattern is really quite basic. A geometric design such as this is often perfect for the homeowner who wants a special look for his deck, without the expense of a craftsman.

This close-up shows in detail how an inlay pattern is set into decking. The cuts require precision measurement and experience working with angles. The design usually requires special blocking on the supporting timbers under the decking. Composite deck materials, such as the decking shown here, are ideal for inlays because many manufacturers offer boards that are a different color on each side—making executing the design much simpler.

Semicircular stairs nestled between walls of foundation skirting is an excellent feature for distinguishing a fairly undistinguished deck. This small, gray dining deck also features natural wood railings with glass inserts, but it's the stairs that set a truly sophisticated tone. This is why choosing stair style is always a part of a good deck design—they should never be an afterthought

Stair configuration goes far in determining how the deck is perceived. Here, a stately staircase of contrasting stained hardwood and white fascia boards follows an "L" run that wraps the staircase around a bland storage unit positioned under the deck. The positioning effectively hides the storage unit and shows off the craftsmanship apparent in details such as enclosed risers and handcrafted post caps.

Handrails on deck staircases are required by many local codes. If you have to include one, you might as well make it a style accent. This ipé handrail has been stained and finished with a gloss coating that shouts chic. The handrail pops even more, framed as it is against balusters in contrasting bright white. Just one more case where safety and style go hand in hand.

A traditional deck calls for a traditional approach to stairs. These steps could have been constructed with open risers (code would have allowed it) but the look would have jarringly contrasted the finished appeal of the rest of the deck. Instead, risers that match the fascia boards, and steps in the same material as the decking, create a very polished look.

When it comes to decks, curves catch the eye, and no more so than when the steps themselves are curved. This type of construction takes a bit more expertise and time, but it pays big rewards in a graceful appearance far beyond what you would expect on such a modest deck. In fact, the scalloped edge is what brings this deck to life, and the stairs are a big part of that flair.

The best deck stairs integrate with the design so that the eye doesn't even necessarily read the steps as steps. The technique used here is a common one on upscale contemporary decks. The steps are built to entirely surround the perimeter of the deck, looking almost like layers or edging. A border of decorative stone adds to the effect and provides a pretty transition between the deck steps and the grass.

The first consideration in designing stairs is safety. But there really is no need to sacrifice style to have safe steps. Here, recessed riser lights provide soft but effective illumination. The two-tone steps are not only pretty, but the variations in color also aids visual depth perception, increasing safety on the stairs. It's a thoughtful design that satisfies both practical and aesthetic concerns.

Often, the simpler the staircase design, the better. This basic staircase allows the beauty of the hardwood to dominate. The handrails are unadorned with flat fillets terminating in rounded edges that are pleasant to the touch. The white enclosure for the risers is apparent next to the steps, but it's a clean look. A separate handrail adds safety, but otherwise, the staircase is handsome without calling attention to itself.

When the terrain calls for a long descent, it's wise to break up the run of a staircase with a platform. A large platform like the one shown here can actually serve as a functional level of the deck, but a smaller platform can be just as effective. The idea is to break up the visual monotony of a long staircase, and to make it easier and safer to climb or descend.

A spiral staircase is a fascinating deck feature and can be a real space-saver as well. The stairs should be carefully designed for optimum spacing, and so that the staircase itself does not steal too much attention away from the deck. Here, the staircase mimics the curves of the deck's outline, and is crafted in the same material, establishing a convincing continuity.

Planters

Planters are natural accompaniments to built-in seating such as benches, because benches can tend to look rather unadorned all alone along the edge of a deck. The most common treatment is to run the bench into a planter as the builder did here. The corner planter is an independent feature. But butting the bench end right up against the planter creates the pleasing visual impression that the two are a single feature.

This multilevel deck illustrates the range of possible built-in planter designs. A foundation planter is nestled next to the stairs that lead to the lawn. Stepped deck-level planters adorn the main deck platform, and a bench-top planter is built into the end of the bench. Use the right planter for the right location and you can create seasonal interest anywhere you need it on the deck.

Handrails are not required by most codes for small, low decks such as this. And although the homeowner could have run the rail all the way around the deck, using built-in features instead provides a visual middle ground between a waist-high barrier and a flat deck. However, a long, uninterrupted stretch of bench might have looked odd; planters are excellent for breaking up spans of long benches.

Just because they blend in nicely with the deck surface and surrounding features doesn't mean planter boxes can't stand out on their own. The planters here have been built with the same composite materials as the decking, but they have been edged in a contrasting natural wood finish that matches an accent stripe running around the border of the deck. The variation makes a more interesting feature out of the planter boxes.

In the end, planter boxes are meant to be planted. The large and deep planter on this small deck provides plenty of space for both abundant soil and water to support a gorgeous profusion of trailing annuals and perennials. The planter sides were crafted to match the angle and material used in the skirting and house siding, making it seem to spring up out of the deck.

Corner planters are wonderfully attractive anchors, off of which you can position other features. The planters here are crafted of the same hardwood as the benches and decking, but stand tall and help define the social corner grouped around a fire pit. The builder has run the boards that make up the planters' sides at a diagonal to make them stand out a bit.

Whether you're creating a planter or other built-in feature, always look for some design flair that will make the feature stand out. This bench is run into the planter, providing anyone that sits on it with the company of lovely flowers. But the designer has added a bit of whimsy by terminating the opposite end of the bench in a point.

Constructing a built-in planter provides the opportunity to create other features at the same time. The designer of this deck didn't settle for a lovely flowering addition to a slotted bench; he extended the planter to create a built-in side table for the bench. The result is a useful and unique feature that perfectly supplements the graceful construction of the bench.

A stunning, sturdy pergola makes its presence known on an elevated dining deck. The pergola was built by an experienced craftsman, and the details show the professional design. Faux footings were created at the base of the supporting posts, and a series of cut-ins decorate the crossbeam ends. Diners benefit from the sun-blocking shade sails—in matching color—draped across the joists.

Composite materials are not only great for decking, they can also make wonderful pergolas. As shown in the details apparent here, composite manufacturers can supply elegant pergola framing members that are finely detailed, durable, and attractive. The white color is a great choice as well, to avoid any fading.

Intricate craftsmanship distinguishes this decorative pergola embellishing the corner of a multilevel deck. Squared, painted columns hold rafters finished natural with ends cut in a wave design. The rafters are crossed on top with decorative members that add an additional layer to the design. A mix of shapes and contrasting colors are design techniques commonly used to create lively and interesting pergolas.

A pergola is the perfect place to show off stylistic flair that can really make a deck stand out. This deck was already special, with a hardwood surface and a pergola roof complemented by posts and balusters painted a very sophisticated gray. The builder added a showstopping centerpiece in the form a pagoda-style topper mounted on the pergola's joists. The effect is at once refined and powerful.

A pergola roof over a backdoor deck shows the potential for drama inherent in the feature. It also shows that pergolas don't necessarily need to be self-supporting; this roof is attached to a ledger on the inside edge, and supported by round, reinforced fiberglass columns on the outside. Both the color and the form of the overhang pop—just as the homeowner hoped they would.

The gaps between the joists of a pergola can create fascinating shadows, but if you're hoping for a two- or three-season deck space, those gaps can be a problem. The owner of this deck solved that problem with clear fiberglass panels attached to the crosspieces that lay perpendicular to the pergola's joists. The space enjoys a wealth of light when it's sunny, and protection from the elements when it's not.

Pergolas are generally dramatic features on any deck, but never more so than when lit at night. This structure is evidence of how spectacular the features look when properly lit. The lighting playing off the varied surfaces of the pergola's support structure and roof creates a wonderful impression that is stage-like in its style.

If you prefer to relax in total shade, away from bothersome insects, a screened gazebo can be the perfect addition to your deck. This one was built from the same ipe hardwood used to construct the deck. By using the same wood on both deck and gazebo, the homeowner unifies the look of the outdoor space, creating an appealing visual continuity.

A gazebo can serve as an exterior room. This was clearly the deck designer's idea in creating this gazebo, with sides that echo the white siding on the house, and a roof made of the same shingles as used on the house. It is an outdoor space that is at once part of the deck and a standalone room where people can sit in more private and intimate surroundings.

The builder put this gazebo off to the side of the deck, but the real separation is achieved by a screened door all its own, and steps leading to the structure. This type of separation requires a lot of planning and you need to be certain that your goal is a standalone room rather than just a slightly intimate area on the deck.

Gazebos are great ways to add splashes to plain decks. This pressure-treated wood deck might otherwise have been rather unremarkable, if it wasn't for a gazebo with a highly detailed, vented bilevel roof. A gazebo roof, especially, can be an area where you can go a bit wild without spending a lot of money. As is apparent here, it's a detail that brings a lot of visual bang for the buck.

A deck gazebo doesn't necessarily have to be round or octagonal. This square version can more than hold its own against any circular rivals. The designer has included decorative exterior corner panels and lattice skirting that surrounds not only the base of the gazebo, but the base of the deck as well. Skirting is a great way to block out the usually unsightly supports necessary to hold up a deck gazebo.

Gazebos

A gazebo can be an excellent way to clearly separate areas of the same deck. This sprawling outdoor surface includes a spa tub with its own platform, an exposed dining area in the center of the deck, and a screened-in gazebo with its own door. Although each area is distinctly different, using the same wood throughout the deck tells the eye that all sections are part of a whole.

A deck gazebo represents the opportunity for the homeowner to dress up the deck. They are almost like tiny room additions. This intricate gazebo features custom balusters, a stacked pagoda roof, and gingerbread trim, all of which adds up to an eye-catching package. Gray lattice skirting helps ground the structure and conceal the support posts that—if apparent—would have detracted from the overall look.

Gazebos are very at home in naturalistic settings, where they can offer a perch nestled right into their surroundings. The gazebo on this deck is situated on a slight peninsula almost on top of a koi pond. The water feature adds a calm and peaceful element to the scene, and no other area of the deck is better situated to enjoy the pond than this covered meditative sitting space.

Gazebos are ideal complements to swimming pools. The structure offers open-air shade from the overwhelming midday sun, and a place to dry off, eat, and relax in between swim sessions. It's essentially a compromise between getting too much sun on the deck, and going inside. This particular gazebo also offers an ideal vantage from which parents can supervise children playing in the pool.

Gazebos

A gazebo doesn't need to be a self-contained room. In the right situation, it can be a minimal and elegant accent. This deck addition is little more than supporting columns and an elegant roof over curving built-in benches. But the style, as restrained as it may be, perfectly suits the simple, traditional design of the rest of the deck.

This is the traditional construction of a pressure-treated wood or softwood (in this case, cedar) deck with an elevated gazebo. Leaving the supporting framework open allows for effective air circulation that prevents moisture-related conditions such as mold or rot. It also lends to easy inspection of the structural timbers for quick detection of any problems that might crop up.

Gazebos are often positioned to sit on their own. But that doesn't have to be the case. The builder of this deck designed a single-level surface, with the gazebo positioned for interaction with the other areas. People enjoying a drink in the gazebo can have a conversation with a group clustered around the stone fire pit, separate but still together.

Traditional open post supports or a skirting-enclosed structure are not the only options for holding up an elevated deck's gazebo. The support itself can be an opportunity for creativity, as this unique deck clearly shows. The gazebo is supported on a one-of-a-kind poured cement foundation that creates its own attention-getting feature.

The gazebo at night, when lit properly, becomes a cozy, welcoming outdoor room. Especially on overcast nights where the stars don't provide a reason for reclining on the deck, a gazebo can offer an intimate space with enough light for socializing, but with the outdoor connection no kitchen or living room can offer.

Fences often serve more than one purpose on a deck. This beautiful, slatted ornamental fence—designed to match the graceful, slim pergola—not only contributes a stunning visual feature to the look of the deck, it also serves as a wind break for the fire pit. The practical application ensures the comfort of this social area while providing a lovely backdrop that creates a sense of intimacy.

This deck would be extremely exposed to the view from neighbors' yards without some sort of screening. Square-pattern lattice effectively blocks prying eyes, while allowing for air circulation and light penetration. Using screens on both sides of the deck is a great idea in situations where the goal is create an intimate feeling for the whole structure.

The owner of this home was dealing with close property lines and wanted a sense of separation from the neighbors' property. The solution was Japanese-style privacy screens created with simple squares of the same stained wood used on the deck, covered with an exterior-grade fabric that is water- and UV-resistant. The result is a magical tiny outdoor hideaway.

Stepped privacy screens are just one of many sophisticated design elements on this large deck. The simple, tight lattice pattern with a top rail flows visually into the elegant railing that follows the gently curved shape of the deck. A large staircase planter box completes the design on the other side. The square lattice skirting mimics the look of the privacy screens and pulls the whole design together.

The spa tub deck shown here was painted gray for a subdued look. But the privacy screen was finished natural so that the fine details of the staggered screen layout would stand out against the deck. Notice the handrails have been left natural as well, to carry through the look of the screen and lead the eye (as well as the visitor) up to the spa tub.

Deck privacy screens or fences don't necessarily have to be intricately designed to be effective. Although lattice privacy screens are the most common type, this simple slatted design is just as effective and quite handsome as well. The slats allow for cooling breezes to flow over the spa tub, taking an edge off the heat of hot summer nights and steamy water.

As lovely as they might be during the day, a row of elegant privacy screens adds a charming element to the nighttime deck. The screens on this deck form a wall along the property line; post-mounted downlights help make the pattern of the latticework pop out. Light bounces off the screening, creating a much more charming and inviting feel than if the deck had been left wide open.

Handsome form meets pragmatic function in the stepped-down privacy screens bordering the outside edge of this softwood deck. The deck's levels cascade into the yard, with the fence providing a visual barrier anchoring the deck design. But more than that, the fence provides maximum privacy for spa tubbing, with solid fencing topped by decorative latticework panels.

Privacy fences often serve a decorative purpose. But screens such as the one used on this deck can be extremely effective at shielding anyone on the deck from an unpleasant view, or from the prying eyes of neighbors. This particular screen allows the homeowner to dine outside without being subjected to a view of the street, or intrusive eavesdroppers.

A cozy backyard deck is the perfect place for a fresh-air breakfast, but not if the neighbors are watching. This simple, plain screen provides a modicum of privacy whether the homeowner is enjoying a weekend summer morning with the paper or hosting an intimate cookout party. The latticework is seemlessly blended with the other deck details because the builder used the same post style as used in the railings on the deck.

Privacy screens can create wonderfully intimate spots on an otherwise open deck. This five-foot-tall screen blocks a view of the street from the side of the deck, and allows for contemplative rocking or a restful hour spent reading away from the rest of the world.

A concrete fire pit is the perfect centerpiece of a cozy corner framed by built-in benches with cushions and pillows. This pit is just large enough to warm and illuminate whoever is sitting on the benches, and it comes equipped with a copper hood that prevents embers from flying up and away. The hood can also be used to extinguish the fire when it's time to go inside.

Fire pits come in all shapes and sizes. Modest braziers simply supply a small flame, but large, ornate units like the one shown here can serve as decorative centerpieces on the deck. Lit or unlit, this is an eye-catching deck feature, with its intricate wrought-metal base. The stone lip can hold a plate of food, a drink, or your feet while you warm them.

The whole idea behind positioning a fire pit on a deck is to make for a comfortable and snug social corner. This homeowner creates the perfect relaxation zone around a basic fire pit, with well-cushioned chairs and benches clustered together. Notice that the pit is covered with a safety screen to keep coals and embers off the composite decking and out of the hillside vegetation.

You can create pleasant conversation circles around a fire pit with furniture or built-ins. Or, as is the case on this wood deck, you can use both for maximum flexibility. The U-shaped built-in benches were crafted specifically to cluster around the fire pit. The ceramic pit is arresting in its own right, and even more so with a lively orange blaze burning in the center.

A spectacular two-level deck provides basic outdoor seating areas upstairs with the entire bottom level focused on a stone fire pit. The white stone perfectly contrasts with the two-tone composite deck and provides an obvious focal point. Built-in seating curves invitingly around the fire pit, and underseat lighting supplements the illumination from the pit.

Where you have the space and budget, a custom-made fireplace is even more impressive than a fire pit. A large brick fireplace is a wonderful focal point for a distinctly autonomous seating area on a large sprawling deck. The fire cuts through any nighttime chill, and is a lovely feature to create the perfect environment for socializing or just relaxing.

If you're after a truly opulent deck, it helps to think outside the box. Rather than incorporate a traditional fire pit in the center of this deck, the builder customized one into the concrete bench. It's a sleek treatment that allows people to cluster close to the fire and still enjoy the built-in seating.

Deck Lighting

The deck at night is a different space entirely. Stars break out overhead and dramatic shadows cloak the landscape. Rather than a platform for sun worshipping, the night deck is reserved for socializing, dining, or enjoying an intimate hour in the spa tub. Whatever you choose to use it for, you'll need to adequately light the deck for after-dark use.

Deck lighting is both a functional necessity and design element. As a practical matter, deck fixtures provide safety and convenience. Lights on the deck are most commonly used at points of transition from one level to another. This includes at the edge of a deck that borders a lawn, and on stairs.

But it also creates a mood that defines the deck after the sun goes down. Deck lighting can create drama, or set a cozy stage. Lighting fixtures themselves can be decorative accents. Although many are recessed or colored to blend into deck structures, you can also choose fixtures that are beautiful day or night. The most popular of these are post cap lights, positioned on the top of railing posts. Solar fixtures are extremely popular, but most fixtures are low-voltage units that are plugged into a deck receptacle. Both can be controlled with a photocell "eye" that detects when the sun goes down and automatically turns on the lights.

Deck lighting is usually in the form of downlights, with the beam projecting toward the deck and out of people's eyes. You may want to include general ambient lighting where the deck is large, although most people prefer to use candles or other various sources of light to retain the deck's romantic allure at night. After all, what's a night deck for if not to enjoy the subtle mystery of a moonlit outdoors.

You'll find that if you use your deck at night, downlights are indispensable. Any light projecting down at the deck surface minimizes slips and stumbles. These rail-mounted fixtures provide a subdued yet effective fan of light. In addition to making for safe movement, the triple beams of these downlights give the setting the dramatic appeal of a stage.

Two of the most useful types of deck lighting fixtures are post mounted and baluster mounted. Post-mounted lights can often be positioned on any side of the post to accommodate your own particular deck design and needs. Baluster lights can be moved where needed anywhere along the length of the railing. In both the examples shown here, the lights are meant to seamlessly blend into the railing, with hoods that match the color and material of the surrounding structure and direct the beam of light down, not into people's eyes.

Deck lights are often part of a larger yard lighting plan. Your choice of fixtures should take into account ambient sourc[e] illumination. This poolside deck incorporates modest fixtures under the handrails, and stair lighting for safety. No other lig[ht] because sufficient ambient light is supplied by the dramatic uplights under the trees, the pool lights, and the light that pour[s] large windows.

Well-lit decks are usually outfitted with several different types of lights that serve different purposes. Here, under-bench lights add a little definition to the edge of the deck, making sure nobody trips over the benches. Stair-riser lights also provide safe passage for anyone walking out onto the lawn from the deck, and a privacy screen light spreads a soft, appealing glow over people enjoying a meal at the table.

anufacturers have answered the need for deck lighting with a wonderful selection of fixture styles. This close-up shows the popular low-
ge recessed lights that can be sunk right into the treads of deck boards. The lights can be used to illuminate a path along the deck or for more
tive applications, whichever you prefer.

Can Use

To ensure safety on any deck with stairs, it's a wise idea to design lighting directly onto the stairs themselves. There are many types of deck-stair lighting, but the most popular are mounted on the riser, the vertical piece separating each step. Riser lights are sometimes recessed or, as is the case on these stairs, they are designed as a hooded fixture. The hood ensures light is directed down where it's needed most.

Deck lighting is a chance to introduce additional artistic or aesthetic accents to your outdoor living area. The owners of this deck chose to add neon strips around the top of gazebo and a privacy fence. The added light doesn't produce much illumination for the deck, but it does add an intriguing splash of color overhead.

Deck lighting fixtures are generally designed to be unobtrusive elements. They should not detract from the overall look of the deck during the day. Miniature recessed under-rail lights, like the one on the bottom of this handrail, light the way on a set of steps with an almost mysterious illumination. This type of hidden light is ideal for a more modern look on a deck that features sleek lines and cutting-edge materials.

The amazing variety of deck lighting fixtures available opens up the potential to use them in new and creative ways. The recessed, low-voltage mini spotlights shown in this deck are most commonly used as staircase lights. But they make wonderful accents when used to light a path across the deck. It's a great way to add some fun and an unexpected element to an otherwise sedate deck design.

Stair-step lighting is even more important where the steps themselves vary in depth. The riser spotlights used on these steps are subtle, but they provide enough light to show the differences in step depths. The extremely subdued post-cap lights also serve as visual indicators of the step-down. Notice that the lighting is all very modest, preserving the quiet mood of an evening on the deck.

Use deck lighting to create a mood as well as for safety. Although post-cap fixtures are usually used on transition posts throughout the deck, the designer of this deck used solar powered fixtures on every post, along with spotlights on the step risers. The spots are connected to the deck's weatherproof outdoor electrical outlet and controlled by an electronic eye that senses when the sun goes down.

Manufacturers have made great strides in providing the homeowner with many deck-lighting options. Some, such as this faux stained-glass post-cap light, add a custom look to any deck and serve as a decorative accent during both day and night. Many, including this one, are solar powered lights that can be installed on virtually any deck post.

A large deck in an area with little ambient light benefits from a mix of accent lighting. This multilevel structure was installed on the side of a home, away from any ambient lights. Consequently, the designer used bright post-mounted lights for general lighting, post-cap lights to mark step downs, and recessed stair riser spots that reveal step depths in the darkness.

When your deck—or even part of the deck—is covered, your options for lighting are greatly expanded. The deck here is partially covered with a peaked roof in keeping with the architectural style of the house. Because the deck is often used for entertaining and relaxing at night, the homeowner chose to use hanging Craftsman-style lanterns to brighten the darkness and add a flash of style to the outdoor room.

Photo Credits

Page 4, Photo courtesy of CA Redwood Association, www.calredwood.org/photo by Ernest Braun

Page 5 bottom, Photo courtesy of CertainTeed Corporation, www.certainteed.com

Page 5 top, Photo courtesy of Trex Company, Inc., www.trex.com

Page 6 top, Photo courtesy of Fiberon Composite Decking, www.fiberondecking.com

Page 6 bottom, Photo courtesy of CertainTeed Corporation, www.certainteed.com

Page 7 bottom, Photo courtesy of Archadeck, www.archadeck.com, (888)OUR-DECK

Page 7 top, Photo courtesy of The Deck & Door Company (www.deckanddoor.com), image by AndyCarruth, Jeremy Sampson & Crew, built by The Deck & Door Company

Page 8 bottom, Photo courtesy of Archadeck, www.archadeck.com, (888)OUR-DECK

Page 8 top, Photo courtesy of TAMKO Building Products, Inc., www.evergrain.com

Page 9, Photo courtesy of CA Redwood Association, www.calredwood.org/photo by Marvin Sloben

Page 10 top, Photo courtesy of Cal Spas, www.calspas.com

Page 10 bottom, Photo courtesy of TimberTech, www.timbertech.com

Page 11 bottom, Photo courtesy of TimberTech, www.timbertech.com

Page 11 top, Photo courtesy of Clemens Jellema, Fine Decks, Inc., www.finedecks.com

Page 12 top, Photo courtesy of TAMKO Building Products, Inc., www.evergrain.com

Page 12 bottom, Photo courtesy of CA Redwood Association, www.calredwood.org/ photo by Ernest Braun

Page 13 bottom, Photo courtesy of TimberTech, www.timbertech.com

Page 13 top, Photo courtesy of CertainTeed Corporation, www.certainteed.com

Page 15 top, Photo courtesy of CA Redwood Association, www.calredwood.org/photo

Page 15 bottom, Photo courtesy of CA Redwood Association, www.calredwood.org/ photo by Charles Callister, Jr.

Page 14, Photo courtesy of CA Redwood Association, www.calredwood.org/photo by Marvin Sloben

Page 16 top, Photo courtesy of CA Redwood Association, www.calredwood.org/ top photo by Ernest Braun; bottom photo by Mark Becker

Page 17, Photo courtesy of CA Redwood Association, www.calredwood.org/photo by Ernest Braun

Page 18 -19, Photos courtesy of 4 Quarters Design & Build, www.4qdb.com

Page 20 top, Photo courtesy of The Southern Pine Council, www.southernpinedecks.com

Page 20 bottom, Photo courtesy of Deck Specialists, www.deckspecialists.com

Page 21 bottom, Photo courtesy of Deck Specialists, www.deckspecialists.com

Page 21 top, Photo courtesy of The Southern Pine Council, www.southernpinedecks.com

Page 22-25, Photos courtesy of Advantage Trim and Lumber Company, www.advantagelumber.com

Page 26, Photos courtesy of Fiberon Composite Decking, www.fiberondecking.com

Page 29 top right, Photo courtesy of Trex Company, Inc., www.trex.com

Page 27, Photo courtesy of Universal Forest Products, Inc./Latitudes Decking, www.latitudesdeck.com

Page 28 top, Photo courtesy of Fiberon Composite Decking, www.fiberondecking.com

Page 28 bottom, Photo courtesy of Rhino Deck, www.rhinodeck.com

Page 29 bottom, Photo courtesy of TimberTech, www.timbertech.com

Page 29 top, Photo courtesy of Trex Company, Inc., www.trex.com

Page 30-31, Photos courtesy of Last-Deck, Inc., www.lastdeck.com

Page 32 -33 Photos courtesy of HandyDeck Systems Inc, www.handydeck.com

Page 34, Photo courtesy of Deck Builders, Inc., www.artistryindecks.com

Page 35 top, Photo courtesy of TAMKO Building Products, Inc., www.evergrain.com

Page 35 bottom, Photo courtesy of Trex Company, Inc., www.trex.com

Page 36 top, Photo courtesy of Fiberon Composite Decking, www.fiberondecking.com

Page 36 bottom, Photo courtesy of TimberTech, www.timbertech.com

Page 37, Photo courtesy of The Deck & Door Company (www.deckanddoor.com), materials supplied by The Deck Store

Page 38 top, Photo courtesy of Advantage Trim and Lumber Company, www.advantagelumber.com

Page 38 bottom, Photo courtesy of The Deck & Door Company (www.deckanddoor.com), images by Andy Carruth, Jeremy Sampson & Crew, built by The Deck & Door Company

Page 39 top, Photo courtesy of Fiberon Composite Decking, www.fiberondecking.com

Page 39 bottom, Photo courtesy of Archadeck, www.archadeck.com, (888)OUR-DECK

Page 40 left, Photo courtesy of Fortress Iron Railing & Fence Systems, www.fortressiron.com

Page 40 right, Photo courtesy of TAMKO Building Products, Inc., www.evergrain.com

Page 41 top, Photo courtesy of Clemens Jellema, Fine Decks, Inc., www.finedecks.com

Page 41 bottom, Photo courtesy of CertainTeed Corporation, www.certainteed.com

Page 42, Photos courtesy of Archadeck, www.archadeck.com, (888)OUR-DECK

Page 43, Photos courtesy of Simpson Strong-Tie, www.strongtie.com

Page 44, Photo courtesy of CertainTeed Corporation, www.certainteed.com

Page 45, Photo courtesy of Fiberon Composite Decking, www.fiberondecking.com

Page 46, Photos courtesy of Clemens Jellema, Fine Decks, Inc., www.finedecks.com

Page 47 bottom, Photo courtesy of Clemens Jellema, Fine Decks, Inc., www.finedecks.com

Page 47 top, Photo courtesy of GAF Decking Systems, www.gaf.com

Page 48 bottom, Photo courtesy of Fortress Iron Railing & Fence Systems, www.fortressiron.com

Page 48 top, Photo courtesy of Clemens Jellema, Fine Decks, Inc., www.finedecks.com

Page 48 top, Photo courtesy of RailingWorks, www.railingworks.com

Page 49 bottom, Photo courtesy of CertainTeed Corporation, www.certainteed.com

Page 50 top, Photo courtesy of Decklighting Systems, www. decklightingsystems.com

Page 50 bottom, Photo courtesy of Deck Specialists, www.deckspecialists.com

Page 51-52, Photos courtesy of Clemens Jellema, Fine Decks, Inc., www.finedecks.com

Page 53 top, Photo courtesy of GAF Decking Systems, www.gaf.com

Page 53 bottom, Photo courtesy of Aurora Deck Lighting, www.auroradecklighting.com

Page 54, Photo courtesy of TimberTech, www.timbertech.com

Page 55 top, Photo courtesy of Clemens Jellema, Fine Decks, Inc., www.finedecks.com

Page 55 bottom, Photo courtesy of The Deck & Door Company (www.deckanddoor.com), images by Andy Carruth, Jeremy Sampson & Crew, built by The Deck & Door Company

Page 56, Photos courtesy of Clemens Jellema, Fine Decks, Inc., www.finedecks.com

Page 57, Photo courtesy of CA Redwood Association, www.calredwood.org/photo by Mark Becker

Page 58 top, Photo courtesy of Archadeck, www.archadeck.com, (888)OUR-DECK

Page 58 bottom, Photo courtesy of Clemens Jellema, Fine Decks, Inc., www.finedecks.com

Page 59 Photos courtesy of Fiberon Composite Decking, www.fiberondecking.com

Page 60, Photo courtesy of Sundance Spas, www.sundancespas.com

Page 61 top, Photo courtesy of Cal Spas, www.calspas.com

Page 61 bottom, Photo courtesy of Sundance Spas, www.sundancespas.com

Page 62 top, Photo courtesy of Cal Spas, www.calspas.com

Page 62 bottom, Photo courtesy of Archadeck, www.archadeck.com, (888)OUR-DECK

Page 63, Photo courtesy of Advantage Trim and Lumber Company, www.advantagelumber.com

Page 64 top, Photo courtesy of CA Redwood Association, www.calredwood.org/photo by Vic Moss

Page 64 bottom, Photo courtesy of Cal Spas, www.calspas.com

Page 65, Photo courtesy of Fiberon Composite Decking, www.fiberondecking.com

Page 66, Photo courtesy of Advantage Trim and Lumber Company, www.advantagelumber.com

Page 67 top, Photo courtesy of TAMKO Building Products, Inc., www.evergrain.com

Page 67 bottom, Photo courtesy of Advantage Trim & Lumber Company, www.advantagelumber.com

Page 68 left, Photo courtesy of CertainTeed Corporation, www.certainteed.com

Page 68 right, Photo courtesy of Clemens Jellema, Fine Decks, Inc., www.finedecks.com

Page 69, Photo courtesy of GAF Decking Systems, www.gaf.com

Page 70 top, iStock

Page 70 bottom, Photo courtesy of Hickory Dickory Decks, www.hickorydickorydecks.com, (800)263-4774

Page 71-72, Photos courtesy of Hickory Dickory Decks, www.hickorydickorydecks.com, (800)263-4774

Page 73 bottom, iStock

Page 73 top, iStock

Page 74, Photo courtesy of TAMKO Building Products, Inc., www.evergrain.com

Page 75 top, Photo courtesy of Deck Builders, Inc., www.artistryindecks.com

Page 75 bottom, Photo courtesy of Hickory Dickory Decks, www.hickorydickorydecks.com, (800)263-4774

Page 76 top, Photo courtesy of Hickory Dickory Decks, www.hickorydickorydecks.com, (800)263-4774

Page 76 bottom, Photo courtesy of Deck Builders, Inc., www.artistryindecks.com

Page 77-78, Photos courtesy of Clemens Jellema, Fine Decks, Inc., www.finedecks.com

Page 79 bottom, Photo courtesy of Deck Builders, Inc., www.artistryindecks.com

Page 79 top, Photo courtesy of Clemens Jellema, Fine Decks, Inc., www.finedecks.com

Page 80, Photo courtesy of Trex Company, Inc., www.trex.com

Page 81 top, Photo courtesy of Archadeck, www.archadeck.com, (888)OUR-DECK

Page 81 bottom, Michal Gerard Construction, www.michalgerardconstruction.com

Page 82 top, Photo courtesy of Clemens Jellema, Fine Decks, Inc., www.finedecks.com

Page 82 bottom, iStock

Page 83 top, Photo courtesy of Clemens Jellema, Fine Decks, Inc., www.finedecks.com

Page 83 bottom, Photo courtesy of TAMKO Building Products, Inc., www.evergrain.com

Page 84, Photo courtesy of Fiberon Composite Decking, www.fiberondecking.com

Page 85, Photos courtesy of Clemens Jellema, Fine Decks, Inc., www.finedecks.com

Page 86 top, Photo courtesy of Clemens Jellema, Fine Decks, Inc., www.finedecks.com

Page 86 bottom, Photo courtesy of The Deck & Door Company (www.deckanddoor.com), images by Andy Carruth, Jeremy Sampson & Crew, built by The Deck & Door Company

Page 87 top, Photo courtesy of Fortress Iron Railing & Fence Systems, www.fortressiron.com

Page 87 bottom, Photo courtesy of The Deck & Door Company (www.deckanddoor.com), images by Andy Carruth, Jeremy Sampson & Crew, built by The Deck & Door Company

Page 88, Photos courtesy of Clemens Jellema, Fine Decks, Inc., www.finedecks.com

Page 89 top, Photo courtesy of RailingWorks, www.railingworks.com

Page 89 bottom, Photo courtesy of Clemens Jellema, Fine Decks, Inc., www.finedecks.com

Page 90, Photo courtesy of TimberTech, www.timbertech.com

Page 91 top, Photo courtesy of Clemens Jellema, Fine Decks, Inc., www.finedecks.com

Page 91 bottom, Photo courtesy of The Deck & Door Company (www.deckanddoor.com), images by Andy Carruth, Jeremy Sampson & Crew, built by The Deck & Door Company

Page 92 left, Photo courtesy of The Deck & Door Company (www.deckanddoor.com), images by Andy Carruth, Jeremy Sampson & Crew, built by The Deck & Door Company

Page 92 right, Photo courtesy of TimberTech, www.timbertech.com

Page 93-99, Photos courtesy of Clemens Jellema, Fine Decks, Inc., www.finedecks.com

Page 100, Photo courtesy of TAMKO Building Products, Inc., www.evergrain.com

Page 101 top, Photo courtesy of Hickory Dickory Decks, www.hickorydickorydecks.com, (800)263-4774

Page 101 bottom, Photo courtesy of TimberTech, www.timbertech.com

Page 102, Photo courtesy of CA Redwood Association, www.calredwood.org / photo by Ernest Braun

Page 103 top, Photo courtesy of Advantage Trim and Lumber Company, www.advantagelumber.com

Page 103 bottom, Photo courtesy of Hickory Dickory Decks, www.hickorydickorydecks.com, (800)263-4774

Page 104 bottom, Photo courtesy of Fortress Iron Railing & Fence Systems, www.fortressiron.com

Page 104 top, Photo courtesy of Deck Builders, Inc., www.artistryindecks.com

Page 105 top, Photo courtesy of TimberTech, www.timbertech.com

Page 105 bottom, Photo courtesy of Universal Forest Products, Inc./Latitudes Decking, www.latitudesdeck.com

Page 106, Photo courtesy of Hickory Dickory Decks, www.hickorydickorydecks.com, (800)263-4774

Page 107, Photos courtesy of Clemens Jellema, Fine Decks, Inc., www.finedecks.com

Page 108 top, Photo courtesy of Clemens Jellema, Fine Decks, Inc., www.finedecks.com

Page 108 bottom, Photo courtesy of Hickory Dickory Decks, www.hickorydickorydecks.com, (800)263-4774

Page 109 bottom, Photo courtesy of Dekor, www.de-kor.com

Page 109 top, Photo courtesy of Hickory Dickory Decks, www.hickorydickorydecks.com, (800)263-4774

Page 110 top, Photo courtesy of Clemens Jellema, Fine Decks, Inc., www.finedecks.com

Page 110 bottom, Photo courtesy of Deck Builders, Inc., www.artistryindecks.com

Page 111, Photo courtesy of Fortress Iron Railing & Fence Systems, www.fortressiron.com

Page 112 bottom, Photo courtesy of Hickory Dickory Decks, www.hickorydickorydecks.com, (800)263-4774

Page 112 top, Photo courtesy of Clemens Jellema, Fine Decks, Inc., www.finedecks.com

Page 113, Photos courtesy of Hickory Dickory Decks, www.hickorydickorydecks.com, (800)263-4774

Page 114 top, Photo courtesy of Clemens Jellema, Fine Decks, Inc., www.finedecks.com

Page 114 bottom, Photo courtesy of Hickory Dickory Decks, www.hickorydickorydecks.com, (800)263-4774

Page 115 bottom, Photo courtesy of Universal Forest Products, Inc./Latitudes Decking, www.latitudesdeck.com

Page 115 top, Photo courtesy of The Deck & Door Company (www.deckanddoor.com), materials supplied by The Deck Store

Page 116 top, Photo courtesy of Clemens Jellema, Fine Decks, Inc., www.finedecks.com

Page 116 bottom, Photo courtesy of Trex Company, Inc., www.trex.com

Page 117, Photo courtesy of Clemens Jellema, Fine Decks, Inc., www.finedecks.com

Page 118 top, Photo courtesy of Hickory Dickory Decks, www.hickorydickorydecks.com, (800)263-4774

Page 118 bottom, Photo courtesy of Deck Builders, Inc., www.artistryindecks.com

Page 119 top, Photo courtesy of Clemens Jellema, Fine Decks, Inc., www.finedecks.com

Page 119 bottom, Photo courtesy of Deck Builders, Inc., www.artistryindecks.com

Page 120 top, Photo courtesy of Advantage Trim and Lumber Company, www.advantagelumber.com

Page 120 bottom, Photo courtesy of Clemens Jellema, Fine Decks, Inc., www.finedecks.com

Page 121 top left, Photo courtesy of Clemens Jellema, Fine Decks, Inc., www.finedecks.com

Page 121 top right, Photo courtesy of The Deck & Door Company (www.deckanddoor.com), images by Andy Carruth, Jeremy Sampson & Crew, built by The Deck & Door Company

Page 121 bottom, Photo courtesy of Clemens Jellema, Fine Decks, Inc., www.finedecks.com

Page 122-123, Photos courtesy of Hickory Dickory Decks, www.hickorydickorydecks.com, (800)263-4774

Page 124 bottom, Photo courtesy of Hickory Dickory Decks, www.hickorydickorydecks.com, (800)263-4774

Page 124 top, Photo courtesy of Trex Company, Inc., www.trex.com

Page 125-129, Photo courtesy of Hickory Dickory Decks, www.hickorydickorydecks.com, (800)263-4774

Page 130, Photo courtesy of Aurora Deck Lighting, www.auroradecklighting.com

Page 131, Photos courtesy of Clemens Jellema, Fine Decks, Inc., www.finedecks.com

Page 132 top, Photo courtesy of TAMKO Building Products, Inc., www.evergrain.com

Page 132 bottom, Photo courtesy of Clemens Jellema, Fine Decks, Inc., www.finedecks.com

Page 133 top, Photo courtesy of Fiberon Composite Decking, www.fiberondecking.com

Page 133 bottom, Photo courtesy of Clemens Jellema, Fine Decks, Inc., www.finedecks.com

Page 134 bottom, Photo courtesy of Archadeck, www.archadeck.com, (888)OUR-DECK

Page 134 top, Photo courtesy of Trex Company, Inc., www.trex.com

Page 135, Photo courtesy of Advantage Trim and Lumber Company, www.advantagelumber.com

Page 136, Photo courtesy of Decklighting Systems, www. decklightingsystems.com

Page 137 top, Photos courtesy of TimberTech, www.timbertech.com

Page 137 bottom, Photo courtesy of Decklighting Systems, www.decklightingsystems.com

Page 138 bottom, Photo courtesy of Trex Company, Inc., www.trex.com

Page 138 top, Photo courtesy of Hickory Dickory Decks, www.hickorydickorydecks.com, (800)263-4774

Page 139 bottom, Photo courtesy of Hickory Dickory Decks, www.hickorydickorydecks.com, (800)263-4774

Page 139 top, Photo courtesy of TimberTech, www.timbertech.com

Page 140, Photos courtesy of Dekor, www.de-kor.com

Page 141, Photos courtesy of Universal Forest Products, Inc./Latitudes Decking, www.latitudesdeck.com

Page 142 bottom, Photo courtesy of Highpoint Deck Lighting, www.hpdlighting.com

Page 142 top, Photo courtesy of Dekor, www.de-kor.com

Resources

Archadeck
(888) OUR-DECK; www.archadeck.com

Aurora Deck Lighting
(800) 603-3520; www.auroradecklighting.com

Azek
(877) ASK-AZEK; www.azek.com

Cal Spas
(800) CAL-SPAS; www.calspas.com

California Redwood Council
www.calredwood.org

CertainTeed Corporation
(800) 782-8777; www.certainteed.com

ChoiceDek
(800) 951-5117; www.choicedek.com

Correct Deck/GAF Decking Systems
(877) 332-5877; www.correctdeck.com

Deck Lighting Systems
(888) 305-4232; www.decklightingsystems.com

Dekor
(800) 258-0344; www.de-kor.com

Fiberon
(800) 573-8841; www.fiberondecking.com

Forest Stewardship Council
(612) 353-4511; www.fscus.org

Fortress Iron Railing & Fence Systems
(866) 323-4766; www.fortressiron.com

HandyDeck/EzyTile
(888) 681-2072; www.ezytile.com

Highpoint Deck Lighting
(888) 582-5850; www.hpdlighting.com

Jacuzzi
(866) 234-7727; www.jacuzzi.com

Last Deck
(866) 527-8332; www.lastdeck.com

LockDry/FSI Home Products
(888) 739-6172; www.lockdry.com

Rhino Deck
(800) 535-4838; www.rhinodeck.com

Simpson Strong-Tie
(800) 999-5099; www.strongtie.com

Southern Pine Council
(504) 443-4464; www.southernpine.com

Sundance Spas
(800) 883-7727; www.sundancespas.com

Tamko Building Products/Evergrain Decking
(800) 641-4691; www.tamko.com

TimberTech
800-307-7780; www.timbertech.com

Trex
(800) BUY-TREX; www.trex.com

United Forest Products/Latitudes Decking
(877) 463-8379; www.ufpi.com